DR. JULIAN HOSP
BLOCKCHAIN 2.0
simply explained - far more than just Bitcoin

1. Edition 2019
© 2018 by I-Unlimited.
8 Hennessy Road
14F China HK Tower
99999 Wan Chai, Hong Kong
team@i-unlimited.de

All rights reserved. No part of this work may be reproduced, translated nor distributed by any means including photocopying, recording or any electronical or mechanical methods without the prior written permission of the publisher, except in the case of brief quotations embodied in critical reviews and certain other noncommercial uses permitted by copyright law. While best efforts have been used in preparing this book, the author and publisher make no representations or warranties of any kind and assume no liabilities of any kind with respect to the accuracy or completeness of the contents and specifically disclaim any implied warranties of merchantability or fitness of use for a particular purpose. Neither the author nor the publisher shall be held liable or responsible to any person or entity with respect to any loss or incidental or consequential damages caused, or alleged to have been caused, directly or indirectly, by the information or programs contained herein. Our views and rights are the same: You are responsible for your own choices, actions, and results. No warranty may be created or extended The operators of respective websites and links mentioned in the book are exclusively responsible for the contents on these websites.

Author: Dr. Julian Hosp
Editor and Translator:
Patricia Zinnecker
Cover design: Ruben Starman
Set: Benjamin Möller

TABLE OF CONTENTS

Foreword By Frank Thelen 12

Identify Opportunities 14
Changes? 14
Waves 17
Yay Or Nay? 19
My Story 21
A Preview 24
For Whom Is This Book Not Suitable? 26
For Whom Is This Book Suitable? 27
Download Tip 29

More Than Just Bitcoin 32
Consensus 34
Decentralization 35
Decentralized Ledger Technologies 37
Blockchain Applications 39
Examples 40

Blockchain In Detail 44
What Is A Blockchain? -
An Explanation In 30 Seconds 45
Which Problem Does A Blockchain Solve? 46
Functionality Of A Blockchain In Detail 54
Cryptography Basics 55
Hashing Algorithms 56
Asymmetric Cryptography 60
Consensus Creation In A Blockchain (Mining) ... 65
How To Create A Blockchain? 69

How To Use A Blockchain?	73
SWOT Analysis	78

The Seven Strengths Of Blockchain Technology — 80

1. Immutability	81
2. Privacy	82
3. Trust	82
4. Compatibility	83
5. Transparency	84
6. Redundancy	84
7. Inclusiveness	85

The Seven Weaknesses Of Blockchain Technology — 88

1. Usability	90
2. Costs	91
3. Waste Of Resources	92
4. Scaling Limitation	93
5. Rigidness	96
6. Privacy	97
7. Personal Responsibility	98

Blockchain Application 1: Ownership — 102

Cryptocurrencies (Financial Sector)	104
Miles And Points (Loyalty Programs, Credit Cards, Airlines)	111
Gaming Token (Computer Games)	114
Media Content (Instagram, Youtube …)	117
Documents (Pdfs, Notarial Deeds Or Contracts …)	119
Registry (Lands, Properties, Real Estate …)	121
Identity (Nationality, Passports, Identity Cards …)	125
Patents And Trademarks (Patent Office, Ip Associations …)	129

Blockchain Application 2: Data Protection **132**

Medicine (Patient Data, Prescriptions,
Vaccination Certificates ...) 132
Communication (Whatsapp, E-Mail, Sms ...) 138
Social Media And Search Engines
(Facebook, Google ...) 140
Data And Passwords (Credit Card Data, Access Data...)... 142

Blockchain Application 3: Smart Contracts **144**

Trusteeship (Notaries, Lawyers, Ebay) 144
Decentralized Computer Programs
(Regulated Platforms...) 147
Betting (Betting Offices, Lottery Offices...) 149
Gambling (Casinos, Poker ...) 151
Oracle   (Expert Opinion, Expert Advice ...)..................... 153
Insurances (Claims, Settlements...) 158
Crowdfunding And ICOs
(Funding Platforms, Private Equity Investments ...) 163
Global Agreements
(Intergovernmental Contracts,
International Court Of Justice) 166
Courts   (Jurisprudence, Courts Of Arbitration) 167
Artificial Intelligence (Clouds, Computers ...) 169
Skynet (Terminator ...) 171

Blockchain Application 4: Tokenization **173**

Securities (Equities, Bonds...) 173
Company Registry (Commercial Registry ...) 175
Real Estate (Apartments, Reits ...) 177
Precious Metals (Gold, Silver ...)..................................... 180

Blockchain Application 5: Transparency **182**

Accounting (Inventory, Tax Consultant…).....................	182
Audits (Iso-Certifications…)	184
Logistics (Supply Chain, Shipping…)	186
Gemstones (Diamonds…)	187
Pharmaceuticals (Medications, Drugs)	189
Copyright Protection (Music, Movies, Programs, Royalties, Digital Uniqueness…)	191
Elections (Electoral Systems, Referenda)	192
Energy (Electricity Supply …)	195
Traffic Improvement (Toll Booths, Avoidance Of Traffic Jams)	197
Donations (Charities, Fundraising)	198
Taxes (Governments)	199
Decentralized Autonomous Governments (States On The Blockchain)	201
Decentralized Autonomous Organisations (Franchise Companies)	203
Decentralized Autonomous Corporations (Non-Profit Organisations, Teams)	207
Reputation (Personal Reputation, Product Quality, Corporate Image)	209
Fake News (Newspapers, Social Media, Blogs)	212
Education Systems (Schools, Teaching…)	214
Curricula Vitae (Certificates, Testimonies, University Degrees)	215
Rating Platforms (Hotels, Restaurants, Forums)	218
DNS-Routing (Internet Provider)	220

Blockchain Application 6: Redundancy **222**
Swarm Behaviour (Drones, Nanobots...) 222
Self-Driving Cars (Tesla, Uber) 226
Indestructible Data
(Information Retention ...) 228
Big Data (Google, Machine Learning...) 230

Blockchain Application 7: Inclusiveness **232**
Freedom Of Speech (Media, Governments) 232
Third World Countries (Finance, Development Aid...) 234
Refugees (Identification, Registration) 236
Internet Of Things (Industry 2.0,
Robots, Smart Devices, Smart Homes) 239
Space (SpaceX, NASA) 242
Entrepreneurship (Startups,
Founding A Company...) 245

Seven Threats To Blockchain Technology **248**
1. Hype 248
2. Scandals 250
3. Regulation 251
4. Quantum Computers 252
5. Artificial Intelligence 253
6. Alternative Technologies 254
7. Benevolent Dictator 255

Blockchain Alternatives **256**
Directed Acyclic Graph (Tangle...) 256
Gossip On Gossip (Hashgraph...) 261

Entrepreneurship: From Theory To Implementation 264

From Problem To Solution 264
Blockchain Or Centralized Database? 266
Blockchain In Startups 267
Blockchain In An Existing Company
Or A Public Institution 272
Initial Coin Offerings (ICOs) 275
Marketing 278
Five Success Characteristics Of An Entrepreneur 281
The Future Of Decentralization 285

Afterword 288

About The Author 292

Further Literature 294

Cryptocurrencies Simply Explained 294
25 Stories For My Younger Self 297

CREDIT

Like my previous books, this would not have been possible without the help and support of a number of fantastic people. On the one hand, I owe great thanks to all the different people from the Blockchain ecosystem who have always enabled me to expand my knowledge through stimulating conversations and profound discussions.

In the following I would like to thank various people, who were essential for this book and its creation:
First of all, I would like to thank my wife Bettina, who knows me like nobody else - and supports me in every situation and always keeps my back free. Just when I need it the most, she is always there and reminds me never to give up. Thank you, Princess!

The same applies to Patricia Zinnecker. No matter if brainstorming, coordination or organization - thank you, Pati, for your constant support in various matters.

I'd also like to thank my wonderful friend Dennis Jacobs. Thanks to your critical feedback, this book has become what it is today. You are truly like the brother I never had. I also thank my family, who is always behind me, no matter what I pursue.

CREDIT

In addition, countless people helped me on my way to finish this work. As I would run out of pages, I unfortunately cannot mention everyone. But this book would not have been written had I not been able to collect all of the experiences or encounters in the past years.

Thank you all!

Yours, Julian
Autumn 2018

FOREWORD BY FRANK THELEN

Blockchain is one of the dominant topics in IT and business. At the same time, there is a lot of uncertainty around this topic.

In many articles and public discussions, the blockchain technology is usually only associated with cryptocurrencies, especially bitcoins, if not equated with them. At the other extreme, it is being promoted as a solution to all the problems that digital infrastructures can pose.

If you take a closer look at it yourself, you quickly notice that many self-appointed or supposed experts spread more half-knowledge and phrases than reliable facts. All the more reason to thank Julian Hosp for making a further contribution with this book to explaining blockchain and cryptocurrencies in a well-founded, and really comprehensible way for everyone and showing what is possible with this technology - and what not.

I myself am sure that the right use of blockchain and distributed ledgers will fundamentally change many areas of our lives and our economy: digital currencies, the trading of company shares, administrative processes, energy trading or the automated processing of contracts (smart contracts), to name just a few.

These upheavals will be disruptive and fundamentally change the industries mentioned. The changes also offer the chance that new Amazons, Facebooks and Googles will emerge. We should do everything we can to make this happen and become home to these new billion-dollar companies.

For this to succeed, however, we must all be prepared to deal openly with this new technology, to recognize and exploit its opportunities - and this is only possible if we understand them. Julian makes an important contribution with this book.

Frank Thelen
Summer 2018

IDENTIFY OPPORTUNITIES

CHANGES?

How necessary are changes? How fast do they happen? Those who think about blockchains and other new developments should be open to change. The example of Nokia, whose company spokesman Kari Tuuti gave the following interview to the magazine **Der Spiegel** in January 2007, shows that these sometimes bring along a rapid, completely unforeseen change.[1]

> **SPIEGEL ONLINE:** Apple enters the mobile phone market. Does that scare you?
> **Kari Tuuti** (company spokesman Nokia): Not at all. We already sell the Nokia N91 with eight gigabyte memory capacity. Apple's iPhone may not be available in Europe until the end of the year. **So, we have a year head start.**
> **SPIEGEL ONLINE:** But couldn't Apple shake up the mobile phone market and endanger Nokia's position?
> **Tuuti:** I trust in our products. And in the new devices that will be launched on the market in the coming months. The iPhone is a serious competitor product.

---

[1] NOKIA (www.nokia.com): Summary of the original source from the interview with Spiegel Online on January 10, 2007 by Nokia's company spokesman: http://www.spiegel.de/netzwelt/mobil/nokia-reaktion-auf-apples-iphone-we-have-a-year-leading-a-458742.html

But I am sure that we will remain the market leader. In the area of multimedia mobile phones, which also includes the iPhone, we sold almost 40 million units last year. **Our market share here is 50 percent, so we're the undisputed number one.**

Only six years later, in 2013, the situation is completely different. After Nokia had been the world's largest mobile phone manufacturer from 1998 to 2011, the **company was replaced by Samsung as number one; Nokia only had a market share of 22.5 percent.** The background: Nokia had **reacted too late to the upheaval in the mobile phone market, which** had begun in 2007 with the introduction of the iPhone and the subsequent rise of the smartphone from a niche to a mass product. **On September 3, 2013, Nokia announced its plan to sell its entire mobile phone business to Microsoft.** Apple then became the most valuable company in the world, inspired by the iPhone and its associated products.[2]

Another example of the impact of change is Blockbuster LLC, which operated a worldwide video rental business and was founded in 1985 in the USA. At its peak in 2004, it had over 60,000 employees and 9,000 businesses worldwide.[3] In 2000, Jim Keyes, Managing Director of Blockbuster, was offered a

---

2 https://www.nytimes.com/interactive/2017/12/05/your-money/apple-market-share.html
3 https://www.ibtimes.com/sad-end-blockbuster-video-onetime-5-billion-compny-being-liquidatedcompetition-1496962

small startup company called Netflix for approximately 40 million USD. That was just 1 percent of the value of Blockbuster, which amounted to 4 billion USD. He turned down the offer with a quote that later became famous: „I'm not interested in Netflix, they are no competition and therefore not even on my radar!"[4] In 2010, a few years later, Blockbuster LLC went bankrupt with just under a billion USD in debt. In 2018 Netflix achieved goodwill of over 100 billion USD - 25 times more than blockbuster ever worth.[5]

These and many other examples illustrate one thing: „The only thing that never changes in our world is the change itself".

As history has shown time and again, nothing and nobody can resist this lawfulness, no matter how big a corporation or even country. But those who believe that such things only happen to companies, but not to individuals, should take a close look at the following example:

In 1870, a then 31-year-old recognized a new trend: oil and its products became more and more important. Regardless of whether as kerosene for lamps or as gasoline for the foreign industry: he understood that this fuel would initiate a new trend. From today's point of view, this trend is clear, but at the time this innovation was equal to what the Internet was

---

4 https://www.cbinsights.com/research/big-compay-ceos-execs-disruption-quotes/

5 https://translate.google.com/translate?hl=en&sl=de&tl=en&u=http%3A%2F%2Fwww.manager-magazin.de%2Funternehmen%2Fit%2F-netflix-jetzt-100-milliarden-us-dollar-%20value-revenue-andprofit increase--a-1189288.html

at the turn of the millennium. The young man founded a company that dealt with the production, transport, refining and marketing of oil. A few decades later his company was the largest company in the world, and its wealth and influence has been passed down through many generations and continues to this day. This empire was created by the fact that a single person recognized a new trend and used the chance for himself, which had a lasting influence on his life as well as that of his whole family. The man in question was John D. Rockefeller and his company was the Standard Oil Company, which still today exists in two parts as ExxonMobil and Chevron. It had been split because of its monopoly status.

WAVES

The examples show that it is not only important to identify new trends. Rather, it is a matter of anticipating them, i.e. identifying the opportunities they offer, preparing for them and then using them. As in the examples of Nokia and Blockbuster, the aim is to avoid one's own downfall or, as in the case of Rockefeller, to build something new. This always reminds me of my ten years as a professional kite surfer, when I was surfing at the best surfing spots in the world. I learned the following very quickly with waves and wind:

Someone who isn't interested in surfing doesn't even pay attention to the wind and the waves. Beginners pay attention to this, but they react too late and usually miss the best waves. Professionals learn to anticipate when the wind and the waves come. They know how to position themselves appropriately to experience the best rides of their existence.

Exactly the same applies to the real world: Most people and most companies either do not recognize new trends at all or do so much too late. They're being overrun by the waves like a tsunami. However, it is not only important to learn to recognize changes like a beginner, but rather to anticipate them like a professional in order to position oneself, one's friends, one's family, one's company correctly and in this way to profit from the new trend or at least not to be destroyed by it.

Another factor to consider, is perhaps not that a trend wasn't anticipated or even actioned late, but instead it was simply ignored. As seen in both examples with Nokia and Blockbuster, it was sheer ignorance and stubbornness into believing the old and ‚foolproof' way is the true way, and nothing will ever replace them.

Their confidence and ego got the better of them, narrowed their vision and made them forget to evolve. Today, for example, the trend is moving away from oil and towards renewable energies. This brings enormous changes and challenges, but also implies opportunities for states, companies and individuals! Like the waves when surfing, all sorts of changes come to us at regular intervals. No wave is the same as another, but you learn even better world by world how to profit from it. The word „profit" does not necessarily only mean financial profit, but it can also mean that one has more fun doing one's own work through a new chance, that one can carry out a work in a healthier way, that one can make better provisions for one's own family, etc.

Many of us can still remember the change through the Internet - the already mentioned example Blockbuster will link this change with something negative. It is now also possible to measure the impact that smartphones and social media have on us - Nokia can definitely sing a lament about it. Numerous other waves are just breaking over us, be it artificial intelligence, drones, self driving cars, robots and much more. Perhaps the biggest wave, however, is one on which many new trends will build because of its advantages: Blockchain.

YAY OR NAY?

Have you heard or read about blockchain? Perhaps by an acquaintance or by the press? Is blockchain what was called „the future technology" in your company? Maybe that's even why you bought this book. Maybe you know cryptocurrencies like Bitcoin, Ethereum and Co. and want to understand what the underlying technology can do. Whatever your reason for doing this, I can already tell you one thing: No matter if media, acquaintances or companies: Although many have an opinion about this new trend blockchain, only very few really have a clue about it.

Maybe you're not really completely convinced of blockchain yet, but bought this book because you're wondering if blockchain technology is just a trend or not. Don't worry, you're not alone. While some talk about the next hype, others talk about a development that will never come: „**All that talk about blockchain and decentralization is shit!**" - Nouriel Roubini, an economic expert who should be familiar with such things.[6]

Other voices say:

„**Blockchain will never scale and therefore never be used.**"
„**Blockchain works in theory - practice looks different.**"
„**Blockchain will be replaced by something else.**"
„**Blockchain is merely a hype that comes and goes.**"

This reminds me of the statements in the past, where people didn't see the enormous effects of oil, the Internet or the iPhone coming. But interestingly enough, those who already recognized the tech opportunities at that time are also those

---

6   http://news.fintech.io/post/102evc9/a-verbal-cryptobrawl-breaks-out-at-milken-over-bitcoins-future

who today see the trend of decentralization through blockchains:

„Blockchain is a technical tour de force" - Bill Gates, Co-Founder of Microsoft and richest man in the world.
Who's right now? In my opinion, the best way to find out for yourself is by reading this book. After reading, you will not only understand blockchain, but you can also seize the opportunities it offers - or you can leave it at that.

MY STORY

Now maybe you're wondering what I have to do with this. Actually, my life story doesn't necessarily lead to writing a book about blockchain. I didn't study finance, economics or programming, but became a doctor after ten years as a professional sportsman. As a trauma surgeon, I wanted to help exactly those people after my doctorate in 2011 who, as an athlete, I had all too often witnessed others serious injuries. After a short time in hospital, however, I realized that I wanted to do something new, and so I moved to Asia in 2012. There I learned a lot about economics, finance and innovative technologies in a real life MBA. In 2014 I met another guy from Innsbruck in Bangkok. He and his buddy inspired me with the concept of decentralization through blockchains. Above all, I was impressed by a forecast from the World Economic Forum, in which some of the smartest people in the world are represented: According to their calculations, just under a decade later (from that point in time), 10 percent of all economic activities were to be handled via blockchains.[7] As a doctor, I had always wondered how patient data could be stored more securely. Blockchain wouldn't be the solution to just this one scenario however, but also for numerous other applications too as you'll find out in this book. At that time, however, I realized that the medical field was not yet ready for blockchain. At this early stage, this new technology would probably be more suitable for the financial sector - in the form of cryptocurrencies. Although I had already heard of Bitcoin, the largest cryptocurrency, from a former patient back in 2011 when I was still a doctor in hospital, I dismissed it as a rip-off because I had not understood the underlying technology of blockchain.

In 2014, I realized the potential. For months I spent time reading into blockchain economy, game theory, cryptography, programming languages and finance theory. Since I did not, like some others in this new field, come from areas related to finance, economics or computer science, I had no prejudices about old or new concepts. Every concept was new to me, and I

---

[7] https://www.weforum.org/agenda/2018/03/blockchain-bitcoin-explainer-shiller-roubini/

was open enough to see the new as an opportunity, not a danger. In 2015, the two guys I met in Bangkok and I started a company in Singapore. We wanted to make all the upcoming blockchain applications accessible to everyone in the simplest way possible via a single platform. We started in the area of finance by linking cryptocurrencies with a credit card and thus making them usable in real life. But the great vision was to add many other decentralized uses. Soon we had external investors and hundreds of thousands of customers. In 2017, we received almost 70 million USD through one of the world's largest ICOs (Initial Coin Offerings).

In addition to the entrepreneurial success, it became particularly important to me to give something back to the community from which we had received so much. I wanted to help the masses understand cryptocurrencies, blockchain and decentralization. That's why I started online communities on Facebook and Reddit, launched YouTube channels and info blogs, which today all rank among the largest in the world in this area. It became my goal to get one billion people *#cryptofit* through all the free info and explanations. I was soon known as an international expert on blockchain and cryptocurrencies, spoke in front of the European Parliament, met Christine Lagarde from the International Monetary Fund, gave interviews on television and gave lectures in front of thousands of people. In 2017, I published my book *Cryptocurrencies simply explained*[8], which became the absolute No. 1 on Amazon, has been translated into more than 10 languages and has sold over 100,000 copies. Even though the focus so far has been more on Bitcoin and Co., I knew that the underlying technology of blockchain would be the real breakthrough. Until then, the time had not yet been ripe for it, and access to this topic was easier via cryptocurrencies than via other applications. In early 2018, however, I realized that the time had come for blockchain without cryptocurrencies, and so I began to explain more and more about blockchain applications beyond the financial space to explain it simply and clear. A wide variety of topics can benefit enormously from blockchain technology. This would include medicine, energy and artificial intelligence to name a few.

A PREVIEW

This book is all about: explaining in the simplest way possible what blockchain is and what the advantages of this technology are

- The question is whether this will actually have a simi-

---

[8] http://www.cryptofit.community

lar influence on our world in the future as computers, the Internet or social media has done. However, you should not only learn to understand these things by reading them, but rather recognize opportunities for yourself and actively use them. Remember this: knowledge is only worth something if it is also applied!

In the blockchain section you will find all the ideas you need to start your own business or adapt an existing one, and which steps are important for a successful implementation. I won't shill any existing ideas or companies as an „insider", but I don't want to look at things superficially either. Rather, I will refer to my own experiences: On the one hand I will describe what helped me as a doctor to become sucessful in a completely different area today, and on the other hand I will report on the manifold things I have already seen in the blockchain space and what seems to work. I will take a critical look behind all those scenes that are often inaccessible to outsiders, and I will present as objectively as possible what has potential and what does not. Only very few people have this approach, but it is all the more important for me personally to set the bar as high as possible.

FOR WHOM IS THIS BOOK NOT SUITABLE

So, for whom is this book not suitable? This question is important because I personally find it terrible to invest time in a book that turns out to be inappropriate. This usually has nothing to do with the book itself, but rather with the fact that as a reader I was not interested in the subject after all. Using the following criteria, you can find out if this book may NOT be right for you:

If you only want to inform yourself about cryptocurrencies, this book will not fit. Only a few pages deal with this topic. This book is mainly about all other blockchain applications except cryptocurrencies. If you want to understand cryptocurrencies in a simple way and make money with them, I can recommend *Cryptocurrencies simply explained*:

If you are interested in the above, you will have much more pleasure in reading that book. If you are looking for a book from which you can learn how to program a blockchain or learn the exact details of cryptography, I can recommend the book *Mastering Bitcoin* by Andreas Antonopoulos. This is not so much about Bitcoin, but rather about the technical aspects of a cryptocurrency and thus also blockchain. I especially made a cryptographic course on YouTube that you can watch for free.

Simply search for "Julian Hosp Cryptography".

Furthermore, this book is inappropriate for people who are not open to innovation. These are often people who love all the things that exist today, but who would have fought these innovations 25 years ago or perhaps even did so: This is about people who believe that everything always remains the same and that there is no need for further training. If you belong to this group, I can recommend the bad seller „Everything stays as it is". Reading my blockchain book, such people suffer at every single page, because it deals with enormously innovative topics such as data storage, smart contracts, transparent processes, security and much more that will change the world in the coming decades.

This brings me to the group of people who, although they are probably still a small minority in 2018, qualify as early movers, a group to which you are also a part of.

FOR WHOM IS THIS BOOK SUITABLE?

This book is meant for all those people who are open to new things: either because they love new things anyway, or because they are afraid of the unknown now and then but know that it is enormously important to always be on the ball.

It is written for people who like things clear and simple - so that you could explain it to a ten-year-old. Not a complex technical joke, but to the point.
True to the motto Steve Jobs onces stated:

> *"That's been one of my mantras — focus and simplicity. Simple can be harder than complex: You have to work hard to get your thinking clean to make it simple. But it's worth it in the end because once you get there, you can move mountains."*

So, if you're wondering why I sometimes use particularly simple terms: This is because the subject of blockchain is complex enough anyway, and I want to explain it to you in such a way that you are also able to explain it to each other. This is the only way this exciting topic can become socially acceptable. So, if you prefer it complex and difficult, you will be disappointed by this book.

Furthermore, this book is aimed at people who do not necessarily want to understand blockchain down to the smallest technical detail. Rather, it is aimed at all those who are more concerned with financial, economic or social impacts. Of course, we will still be looking at technical content again and again. The reason for this is quite simple: Even though I myself am a technically adept person, I know very well that only a few percent of the population belong to this group of people. Most people simply have other interests than technology. However, it is close to my heart that not only a few technology freaks benefit from blockchain technology, but all those who are open to get to know it.

Last but not least, one thing is important to me: I will always ask you to do something yourself - either as an entrepreneur or as an employee. If you're not really interested, I'll do it anyway. I hope I've given you enough inspiration by the end of the book. Clever people who are committed to decentralization are more necessary than ever. Because as you will learn on the following pages, there are currently more unsolved than solved problems - and I hope that you can provide the decisive breakthrough here or there to enable a more decentralized world in the future.

If you find yourself in only one of the points, then you will have more than just a lot of fun with this book.

DOWNLOAD TIP

Before you start reading, here is an important download tip: A lot of things in this area move with enormous speed. Even as I'm writing this book, there are always new possibilities. Exclusively for readers of this book I have created an up-to-date list with details, videos, blogs and further reading literature, which is much easier to update than an entire book. In addition, I list all links from this book. Especially in the case of a printed publication or an audio book, you cannot simply click on a link. It is therefore much more user-friendly to receive the relevant information digitally. If you want this information as a free bonus to your book, go to www.morethanjustbitcoin.com and get the latest version.

And another tip: new unusual things always feel a bit strange at the beginning. We humans love the familiar. No matter how unpleasant it may feel - try to make a judgment on all the ideas presented here as late as possible. Do not read the passages in question by approaching them with prejudice right from the start. Remember: a wrong opinion can destroy your company in the worst case. A good decision can have a positive effect on your life and that of your offspring - just like Rockefeller did.

Be like a well-functioning parachute: open!

Have fun becoming #cryptofit!
Yours, Julian

MORE THAN JUST BITCOIN

It doesn't matter if you look at objective statistics on Google or if you ask people subjectively for their opinion on what is better known - Bitcoin or blockchain. The answer is clear[9]: Some people know the online currency Bitcoin. But this cannot be said of the underlying blockchain technology. Quite the opposite: Only a few have ever heard of it, and of all those who already know blockchain, only a few can explain what it is. Bitcoin is known to most people as a digital object of speculation, which has made some people very wealthy. Therefore, it is easy to describe why blockchain is much less known than the cryptocurrency - even if it is much more than just a bitcoin.

People prefer to talk about things they understand. Something like blockchain, which you can't touch or buy, isn't so well suited as a report topic in the press or as a discussion topic at the regulars' table. You cannot touch Bitcoin, but you can at least buy as an online currency. This, in turn, permits sensational press releases such as from the 18-year-old Bitcoin millionaire, who as a teenager secretly created the cryptocurrency on his own computer by mining[10], or from the British publications, who tell of a man who threw

---

9   https://trends.google.com/trends/explore?q=bitcoin,blockchain
10 https://fee.org/articles/meet-the-teenage-dropout-who-became-a-bitcoin-millionaire/

away his hard drive with tens of millions of USD worth of bitcoin in a dump[11].

All this helps to make Bitcoin more popular. But in the process, they forget: The same concept that makes Bitcoin so successful in the area of finance could be incorporated into many other areas, creating even greater added value. For example, energy authentication and provision by blockchain could become much more transparent, and electricity could become much cheaper. But that's much more complicated to explain. And it's not as easy for everyone to grasp the process of investing 100 USD in bitcoin and hoping to get rich overnight.

    This chapter is intended to provide a first relief for blockchain beginners. On the one hand it should give a good overview of some technical terms and on the other hand it should explain blockchain technology in the simplest way. In the following chapter, we will go into detail about the individual sub-items of a blockchain.

To start with all this, we have to start with a very banal question: Who actually decides what happened and what didn't? What is considered a fact and what is not? Here we are talking about the so-called consensus.

---

11 https://www.wired.co.uk/article/bitcoin-lost-newport-landfill

CONSENSUS

> *Consensus is agreement on what happened and what didn't.*

At first glance, we often believe that the events are quite clear after all. Only one thing happens, and the other doesn't happen. But anyone who has read George Orwell's 1984 classic knows that the creation of contradictory facts is not only due to a multiverse theory. If we're going to have to deal with the consensus as a phenomenon, we recognize: We are used to governments, companies or important people deciding what happened and what did not happen. The events are thus decided centralized - for example by a person, company etc. Internet companies store our data, or they do not. As you often hear in the news, we as citizens have very little influence on this. News companies write the story in one way or another, and we then take the written as a fact, without realizing what actually happens through such manipulation. A country confirms your identity in your passport, and those from the „wrong" country then have no opportunity to identify themselves. A bank has your balance of thousands of USD at its disposal - or can simply block your account overnight. Then you have to act to get your money back. We don't have a consensus created by a lot, but created by only a few.

This has some important advantages: Consensus creation

(i.e. centralization) is efficient because misunderstandings seldom occur. In a centralized system, there is no danger that two things become reality simultaneously. But with centralization, we are facing a huge disadvantage, and that brings us to the next important term: decentralization.

DECENTRALIZATION

> *Decentralization is the opposite of centralization and means that something, such as power, control or trust, is not given to a sole centralized source, but is instead distributed among many or even all.*

Decentralization is exactly the opposite of what the already mentioned examples of centralized action show: Not a single person is in power, but the participants themselves decide what happens and what does not. Similarly, just as the president cannot simply appoint himself in a democracy, but is elected by the people, that is by many, so this concept can also be applied in a modified form to things such as data storage, possession, identity, communication and much more.

For many people, the concept of decentralization is still as new today as the „Internet" concept was almost 20 years ago. With decentralization, it is not the government of one country that confirms the identity of the citizens in a centralized way, but all citizens confirm the identity of all others in a decentralized manner. This means that everything does not start from a single centralized institution but is decentralized. Everybody's contributing a little bit. In a decentralized system, Google or Dropbox do not store our files centrally, but each user stores the data of each other in a decentralized way. A contract between two parties is not stored in one single place, but is stored locally by anyone else who also wants to conclude a contract. This is called a smart contract.

In the later chapters, we will cite many more examples that illustrate the numerous advantages of decentralization: Trust, power and control flow away from a few to all participants. Not only will this have drastic effects on many aspects of our daily lives, but it will also raise many questions about power relations around the world. At the same time, however, it also becomes clear that decentralization will require a much higher level of data processing for all participants. Computers that can store and process such processes much more efficiently than any procedure without EDP.

And so, we come to the concept of decentralized ledger technologies.

DECENTRALIZED LEDGER TECHNOLOGIES

> *A decentralized ledger is a digital database which is stored by a group of people and kept on the same level in time blocks.*

A ledger is nothing more than a database containing information. A centralized ledger is therefore managed by a centralized party, which has control over the information it contains and can therefore only determine what is or is not stored in it. As mentioned earlier, a centralized system is usually efficient, fast and cost effective, but there is inevitably the problem of centralization and thus of trust. In the decentralized ledger, however, the information in the file is not controlled by a single person or company, but by all participants as a community. In a centralized database, two contradictory facts can never happen, because there is only one party that processes the database. However, anyone who has ever worked together in a group on a Word document or in Google Docs knows that it is much more difficult to keep a database on a uniform footing that several people can „tinker with". However, as a user you do not need to rely on a single person for this.

To avoid misunderstandings during a data update in a decentralized system, a decentralized ledger is not simply updated at will, but the update follows certain rules.

The best-known decentralized ledger technology is a blockchain. The update of the decentralized file functions by the fact that the participants of a community agree in regular time blocks on what happened in a time block of for example ten minutes. When the majority has agreed on the new data entry, this is recorded as an information block in the file and attached to the previous information block of the file. To put it simply, the last entry of the previous block is also the first entry in the next block. One speaks of the fact that a block is cryptographically chained to another block - hence the term blockchain. After each participant has saved the file, everyone knows which consensus has been created. So, no participant can cheat another and for example change the past. It is also impossible to take something away from someone that the person has received. The blocks are attached to each other and therefore unchangeable, because as soon as you change a block, one link of the chain breaks and the whole blockchain is broken.

Consensus in a blockchain can only be changed by exchanging the entire community and the new community agreeing on a new consensus. The more participants there are the less likely it is to be.

A blockchain is therefore nothing more than one of the possible ways of generating consensus decentrally in the digital world. However, there are also other possibilities, such as a tangle or a gossip-on-gossip protocol. We will take a closer look at this in the next chapters, but I would like to give you a rough overview of the concept before I go into more detail afterwards. If we now move on to the next point, we ask ourselves what exactly is stored in such a discreet database - here we come to the different blockchain applications.

BLOCKCHAIN APPLICATIONS

> *Cryptocurrencies are currently the most popular blockchain application.*

So, if we speak of the next level on the path of consensus creation by decentralization using blockchain, to finally arrive at Bitcoin, we come to the penultimate step for the different blockchain applications. These make up the bulk of this book.

Many other blockchain applications can also be easily understood on the basis of cryptocurrencies. Instead of leaving control of the money to a central bank, the information required in the monetary system is stored decentralized on the blockchain. This information includes information such as who owns how much money, who sends how many coins to whom, and how much money actually exists in total. Since each participant stores the blockchain, i.e. the decentralized file with the entire information, on his own computer, everyone can transparently view the information and ensure that no nonsense is done. Cryptocurrencies belong to a large group of applications of a blockchain. They represent one of approximately 50 different blockchain applications currently in existence. They all build on the same advantage and yet each one of these are implemented in different ways.

EXAMPLES

I want to come back to the example of possession of cryptocurrencies: Bitcoin is by far the best-known cryptocurrency and therefore also the best known blockchain application. But maybe you've heard of Ethereum, Ripple, Dash or some others. They all build on the same advantage of their common category, namely the immutability of a blockchain, through which possession can be clearly defined. By using different algorithms, however, the individual cryptocurrencies each define differently, for example, how many coins there are, whether there is a maximum, how to send a coin, whether this coin has a further benefit, etc. The individual cryptocurrencies are thus all different application examples for a similar idea - to make money digital and decentralized. In the field of cryptocurrencies alone, there are thousands of application examples. How many of these will actually be needed in the future remains to be seen.

Of course, the same applies to all other 50 or so applications: Let's take a look, for example, at how blockchain can be used in medicine, in a messaging tool for even more secure forwarding, or in social media for data protection. One can quickly see that there will be thousands of examples here alone. Smart contracts, i.e. automatic contracts on a blockchain, can be used in the form of a decentralized computer such as Ethereum or as a transparent casino and also in many other examples.

Over the course of this book we will discuss all the different areas in which I currently see enormous potential for blockchain. However, I will be holding back with this fifth step of examples, because it is very difficult to foresee exactly what will happen in the various areas. The question I just posed, how many cryptocurrencies are really necessary, is considered the best example for a „The winner takes it all" concept, with which from today's thousands of cryptocurrencies in the future perhaps only a few will prevail. In order not to fall into the trap of betting on weak horses or to highlight dying examples, I will clarify developments in detail that I am convinced will come: the various areas themselves. It's up to you to stay up to date, hopefully start your own company in the field or rely on winning companies and jump off dying ones.

Understanding the route taken so far is essential for understanding blockchain:

> *Consensus → Decentralization → Blockchain → Cryptocurrencies → Bitcoin*

But in the future there will be many other and even more important applications instead of cryptocurrencies. If these are increasingly pushed to the surface, it is all the more essential not to lose sight of the bigger picture. That's what this chapter helps you with.

Before we dive deep into the construction of a blockchain, we'd like to remind you once again to download the latest updates and links so that you don't miss anything from this fast-moving area in this chapter:
www.morethanjustbitcoin.com

BLOCKCHAIN IN DETAIL

"If you can't just explain it simple, you haven't understood it well enough."

Albert Einstein

In this chapter we will look at the concept of a blockchain in detail. However, I will continue to explain things as simply as possible so that you can do something very important: to explain them to someone else as well or to be able to distinguish fact and fiction from each other immediately if you get incorrect contributions on the subject of blockchain in the press, on the Internet or in a conversation, which unfortunately (too) often happens. Let's start with what we stopped with in the previous chapter: explaining a blockchain in less than 30 seconds.

This, by the way, is always the test for me with self-proclaimed „experts": „Can you explain to me what a blockchain is?" Pseudo-expert: „Of course!" „In less than 30 seconds. Without to use ‚decentralized'?" Pseudo- expert: „Umm, no." So that's how you become a true blockchain expert:

WHAT IS A BLOCKCHAIN? - AN EXPLANATION IN 30 SECONDS

"A blockchain is a digital file in which the same information is stored by all members of a community and updates are attached to the existing information in regular blocks of time so that each participant has all the information and does not have to rely on others."

Julian Hosp

If you'd like to know a little more detail:
A blockchain is a digital file which contains data of a community. Each group member is equal, and no one can decide for others. To join the group, one copies this file from another participant and will have all the information. This way everyone has the same file at all times and no misunderstandings can occur, all files are regularly updated with new information. Thereby, everybody knows from his own file whether a statement about the content is correct or not. Since these updates take place in time blocks and are chained together in the file, such a file is called a blockchain.

Now that we have continued with the previous topic, we start with the details of blockchain. Therefore, we have to start with the question, why Blockchain technology was created at all, or in other words, which problem is solved by a blockchain.

WHICH PROBLEM DOES A BLOCKCHAIN SOLVE?

> *A blockchain solves the problem of how a community can store digital information unchangeably without a centralized administration.*

The reason why it is so important to first look at the problem is because only then the solution becomes easily comprehensible. As an example look at the following formula:

$$X + Y = 10$$
What's X, what's Y?

You will agree with me that there are many solutions to this problem, for X and Y. For example, a sum of 10 results in $1 + 9, 2 + 8, 3 + 7$, etc., and that does not even include the numbers with a decimal. But what about the following problem (this is not a trick question)?

$$6 + 4 = ?$$

The solution is simple. It's 10. What's that about? With the first mathematical problem (X + Y = 10) we are given the solution, which has infinitely many starting possibilities. The second (6 + 4 = ?) has a single problem with a single solution.

These two mathematical problems reflect much in our world. A large number of unsuccessful companies or providers of products and services know only too well what they would like to do. Example: "I have a blockchain here. Now I have to find a problem that fits this solution." However, since there are often many factors in our world that influence a potential solution, and since there are always competitors, these unsuccessful companies and vendors will not find anyone to buy their product or service. Of course, something can happen in the short term, but in the long term such a product has no benefit and disappears from the market again.

A good example of how to do it right is Apple. When Apple in 2010 wanted to launch the iPad on the market, every analyst and expert wrote it off in advance as a failure.[12] Parallels were drawn to countless previous floppy developments, and Apple was predicted to have a bleak future. However, marketing expert Steve Jobs knew what he had to show people: NOT the solution, the iPad, but the problem it would solve. And that's exactly what he did when he showed the world how many people actually only wanted to

---

12 https://www.infoworld.com/article/2683548/laptop-computers/why-apple-s-rumored-itablet-will-fail-big-time.html

surf the Internet, look at pictures on Social Media or read an e-book - and people didn't do this on a fixed computer at the desk, but comfortably on the couch, in bed or on the bus. The mobile phone was too small, a laptop too big, too heavy and too inflexible. At that moment, millions of people could identify with the problem and knew that there was no good solution. Now they all wanted a solution: something bigger than a smartphone, but smaller and more portable than a computer. And - tadaa! - Steve Jobs had the solution ready. Apple recognized the opportunity and is riding this wave until today, because so far this solution has sold almost 350 million times.[13] Apple only had to solve the task 6 + 4 figuratively speaking. If one compares Apple with Google, one recognizes the different approaches: While Apple usually starts with the problem in mind to find a solution, Google tends to start with a solution and then tries to find a suitable problem. That's why Google has so many products and services that don't ultimately achieve success. But since the Google developers send a lot of projects into the race, enough are always successful. Google can afford this because the company originally started with a problem for which Google has found the perfect solution: „How to cope with this chaos of the Internet? So, Google is the exception and not the rule. Far too many people don't realize that, but often come to me

---

13 https://www.statista.com/statistics/269915/global-apple-ipad-sales-since-q3-2010/

with: „Julian, I would like to do XYZ in my life - how do I find customers who buy it?" These people are doing exactly the same thing as Google, but they don't have the leeway this giant has. They come up with the solution of 10 and are now looking for X + Y. As soon as they find a problem (X), there are usually already competitors, and whenever they adjust something, the variables change. At some point they think they have found a target group, but later they realize that their product or service is no solution to any real problem. No wonder the plan didn't work out.

So, remember the following for the coming chapters as we go through the different blockchain applications: Before you ask yourself what an application does, ask yourself what problem it should solve! And then ask yourself whether the problem in question is really an actual problem or just an artificially created one that doesn't exist. Without a real problem there is no reason for a solution, but at most a short-term hype. This is exactly the issue of most blockchain applications. Everyone only talks about what these innovations are supposed to do, but only a few talk about the problem they are supposed to solve. There are therefore many misunderstandings in the press and among supporters and opponents of these digital currencies. They don't know if it's just a bubble that's about to burst or if it's the solution to a problem that's going to change the world. We started this chapter with the solution. Let's now talk about the problem where the only solution is a blockchain or even more broadly a decentralized ledger technology:

How can digital information be stored in an unchangeable way without a centralized power of authority?

The basic problem in the digital age is that information can be increased, changed or destroyed practically free of charge. I can save the same photo 100 times and upload it, and this multiplication costs me practically no more than the time to do it only once. Multiplying physical items is either difficult or even impossible. If we save a contract in a Word file, I can easily change it afterwards. With a contract on paper, it's not as simple as that. Even by accidentally pressing the wrong button, I can irrevocably delete a file from the computer within seconds. Trying to make an object in the physical world simply disappear is not that easy.

This is precisely why, when we are in the digital realm, there is always a centralized party that creates consensus. Be it a bank that manages our Internet banking, a centralized service that stores our online signatures, or centralized clouds that secure our data. As soon as you're in the digital domain, there's a central point that's the override. It is important to keep in mind that nobody simply creates, changes or deletes information in this way. With this activity, all centralized institutions enjoy our undivided trust, for they have control over the consensus. Facebook, for example, can delete your data or not. Another example: Only the bank can transfer money to your account, you cannot. The bank can also freeze your money. Since then, people have been asking themselves the question again and again:

„What could a system for digital information processing look like WITHOUT a centralized institution?" Such a system would be open to anyone. There would be no censorship. No company could simply close the account of any user or change it unsolicited. Never have to trust anyone, because everyone would be in control. To hack such a system would be practically impossible, since one would have to change all participants.

Anyone who has ever had a problem with digital information can identify with the aforementioned examples. So before moving on to the next chapter, consider briefly whether you consider this problem of „centralization" to be real and relevant, and if so, how you would solve it.

Let's look at examples from history where decentralized databases have been used before.

Already at the time of the ancient Egyptians there was the concept of the clay tablet, on which for example possessions and property were recorded. If there had been only one clay tablet, this would have been a centralized system. Although the Pharaohs wanted to remain in control of the data, they understood the danger of breaking or loss of these tables. So, they had numerous copies of each plate made, to be stored at different places in the empire. The appointed supervisors met at regular intervals in order to update the clay tablets and avoid information conflicts. The boards were stored decentralized, but only an authorized person was allowed to change them. Therefore, it was no problem to make sure that the correct entries were made even with a large number of people. All this was the responsibility of the pharaoh or his confidants. Although the Pharaoh was still responsible for the information storage, the Egyptians could be relatively sure that once a contract concluded, a purchase of land or a deed would not simply be ruined by a destroyed clay tablet.

On the island of Yap in the South Pacific, a system came into play that was even more advanced in terms of decentralization. However, it only worked because the island community was quite small. The system was that of the Rai stones. The islanders wanted to set up a decentralized system of ownership that would not give anyone on the island a higher status and would not give anyone the opportunity or the right to take care of everyone else's property. So, they began to make huge round stones, which were then used as money. Theoretically, every islander could have made these stones himself, but most of the time it became a specialized task carried out by a few, while those who preferred to receive such stones as payment rather sold products or services in return. Thereby, the system was open to anyone, everyone had the same rights, and no one was worth more or less than anyone else in the Yap Island community.

It was, however, a nightmare to transport these stones from one place to another, as they were deliberately made large to make production more difficult so that they were scarce. The solution? Instead of transporting the stones, the islanders began to store the stones in specific places such as in front of a church, in front of a certain house, etc., and then transferred the possession of the stone to the people who paid for it. Only the knowledge about the transaction process informed everyone else on the island to whom he had just given one of the Rai Stones. So NOT the stone itself was passed on, but the knowledge about who possessed the stone. The stone itself always remained in the same place. Everything was based on a decentralized system where every islander knew who actually owned a particular stone. No one could simply steal a stone, because it was no longer about the stone itself, but about the entire knowledge of the ownership situation in the small community.

However, this concept of decentralization only worked because it was a small group that carried out the exchange of information. Every participant knew everyone else, so there was no need to write down the updates or authorize them if anyone wanted to update. Digitalization, however, affects the entire world, and in a digital world it is not enough just to remember updates.

So how was it possible to create a decentralized system in the digital world?

After many of the necessary building blocks had already been created, the final implementation of the solution took place in 2009: the decentralized Ledger Technology (DLT), and to be precise: the creation of the first real blockchain. To repeat the 30-second definition again:

A blockchain is a digital file that contains data of a community Each group member is equal, and no one can censor data management. Thereby everyone has the same file at all times and no misunderstandings can occur, while everyone updates him- or herself with information regularly. This way everyone knows on the basis of his own file whether a statement is correct or not. To join the group, one copies the existing file from another participant and has all the information. Since these updates are in blocks of time and are chained together in the file, this is called a blockchain.

FUNCTIONALITY OF A BLOCKCHAIN IN DETAIL

> *A blockchain is a decentralized and mostly public database in which processes are recorded by cryptographic hashes as Merkle trees across many computers, so that the data records cannot be changed retroactively without putting in the same energy again that was needed to create the hashes.*

This is the "geeky" definition of a blockchain. It already contains many technical terms, which we will go through now, when we describe the exact function mode of a blockchain. The building blocks of a blockchain have all been around for quite some time. With a blockchain, they are simply reassembled. Communication between individual parties works via the Internet. In order to store all possible information in a file unchangeably, this information must be made „storable" and „unique". Only in this way can this information be stored unchangeably in a blockchain. This requires cryptographic mechanisms, which are also used in many other areas. Neither the Internet nor data storage or cryptography are anything new. Most people are familiar with both the Internet and data storage. For many, however, cryptography is something rather unknown so far. So, in order to understand blockchain in detail I have made the next chapter as clear and simple as possible for you to take a trip into cryptography.

CRYPTOGRAPHY BASICS

In blockchain there are two cryptographic methods that are mainly used, which are also used in many other IT areas: hashing to transform information into a unique combination of numbers and letters, and private-public-key pairs to allow or deny authorizations for data entry.

HASHING ALGORITHMS

With the emergence of digital information in the 1990's, mathematical algorithms were developed to transform any information into a random but calculable combination of letters and numbers with a fixed length. It is important that the sequence from the original information to the hash (the combination of letters and numbers with a length defined from the beginning) is very easy for everyone to perform, but at the same time it is impossible to get from the hash to the original information. Furthermore, it is important that a small change in the original information leads to a completely different and unpredictable hash.

MD5 was one of the first algorithms of this kind, but today it is known as „broken". The biggest issue was, that this algorithm made it easy to recalculate the original information on the basis of the hashes, and that hash collisions occurred. Hash collisions occur when different inputs lead to the same hash. The hashing algorithms have been developed further and today the algorithms from the SHA family are mostly used, the abbreviation stands for „Secure Hashing Algorithm". Blockchain mainly uses the SHA256 algorithm, which „hashes" an input into a binary output with 256 digits.

If you now think that it must be impossible to be able to represent all possible inputs by 2^{256} outputs, then the following fact might change your mind: If every human being in the world would channel billions of inputs through this algorithm, then they would all need more time than how long the entire universe has already existed, in order to be able to present all possible outputs. So, it well could be, that hash collisions exist. However, from today's point of view, SHA256 is currently considered to be safe as they occur with a negligibly low probability. This is similar to the statement that when you shuffle a deck of 64 cards, you are likely to create a combination of cards that has never existed before in history. There are simply too many possibilities in both examples. With SHA256, any information can be represented uniquely as a combination of letters and numbers.

Here are a few examples of a SHA256 hash:

> hello world →
> c615784ccb5fe5936fbc0cbe9dfdb408d92f0f

If you write the „h" and the „w" in large letters, the result is totally different:

> Hello World →
> d7beb04eb7549ce990fb7dc962e499a27230

If you add an exclamation mark or a comma, the output will change completely again:

Hello World! →
7ee4631b9b30ac2754b0ee0c47e161d3f724c

Hello, World →
f9a818abc3da35d745a803d72a660c9f5

You see: It's completely impossible to infer from the input to the input, and even a slight change of input leads to a completely different hash output. The important thing about these algorithms is that they are accessible and visible to everyone (open source). This is the only way to ensure that everyone can theoretically understand and try out these things for themselves. If you are technically experienced, you can take a look at Bitcoin's open source algorithm here and hash your own input:

https://en.bitcoin.it/wiki/Block_hashing_algorithm.

If you would like more information, go to Google and search for „Julian Hosp Cryptography".

With these algorithms, information like „person A sends 3 coins to person B on January 1, 2018 at 10:39 a.m." can be clearly represented as code (hash). If you just change the hash a little bit, the original information would be completely useless. So, it wouldn't just be person A who sends the coins to person C, but the hash would suddenly be about ten camels, for example, who go on a desert hike. A blockchain consists of nothing else but unchangeable hashes, which represent original information. Since each time block in a blockchain stores several updates simultaneously, these hashes are again hashed to a single hash, which is then called the merkle root (hash tree) or block. The different blockchain applications such as contracts, identification data or ownership then result from the question of what the original information consists of, which is hashed to the respective blocks. In this way, financial information becomes cryptocurrencies, contracts become smart contracts, and so on.

Since each participant of a blockchain has equal rights, a further cryptographic mechanism is needed, which ensures that not everyone can simply arbitrarily create, change or delete information, but only someone with the respective authorization keys.

This works via asymmetric key pairs. More about this in the next section.

ASYMMETRIC CRYPTOGRAPHY

Keys in cryptography are used to securely encrypt messages. Until not too long ago, symmetric keys were used for this purpose. The key is the number of steps by which a message is encrypted. This is referred to as symmetric because the encryption and decryption are based on the same amount. For example, you move each letter of a word one position forward. A then becomes, for example, B, B becomes C and so on. The word „fish" then becomes „gjti".

To make this more vivid, imagine symmetric cryptography as a box with a lock. The message you want to send is placed in the box and locked with the key. On the one hand, you have the key to lock it yourself and on the other hand, every person you want to give this message to has the public key so that they can unlock the lock. Since these are the same keys in each case, this is called symmetric. The concept is very simple, but such symmetric keys have some disadvantages. First you have to send the key to the recipient, otherwise he cannot decrypt the message. The transfer of the key would then be a point of attack and thus a vulnerability. In addition, attackers potentially find it easier and easier to decrypt a message the longer the same key is used, because the encryption method (e.g.: always shift a letter) can be cracked at some point.

ASYMMETRIC CRYPTOGRAPHY

To work around these problems, cryptographers discovered asymmetric keys to encrypt messages. This works by first creating a secret private key and then generating a corresponding public key using a mathematical formula. Similar to the hashing functions, it is very easy to calculate the public key from the private key. However, it is practically impossible to execute the reverse function and generate a private key from a public key. An easy to understand example would be the mathematical function of exponentiation and its inverse function, root extraction. While it is relatively easy to square 13 (private key), it takes much longer to calculate the square root of 169 (public key). Asymmetric key pairs, as they are used today, are of course many times more complex, as you will soon find out.

The two keys allow a message to be encrypted with one key and decrypted with the other key. After you have created the public key from the private key, you make the public key public and keep the private key secret.

Think of these asymmetric keys as a special lock that soley only have the position A ("closed") and position B („open"), but after position B („open") another „closed" position C. The sequence would therefore be:

Position A („closed") ◄► Position B („open")
◄► Position C („closed").

We speak of asymmetric keys because the private key can only move the lock from A to B to C and the public key can only move the lock the other way round from C to B to A.

Note that the lock can only be opened in the B position. This works because of the mathematical relationship between the two keys. If you now place a message in the box while the lock in position B is open, and use the public key that everyone has, you move the lock to the closed position A. Now only the person who has the private key can move the lock back to the open B position and read the message. In cryptography it is said that the public key encrypted the message and the private key decrypts the message. However, there is another function, the signing of a message. If you put a message in the box in the open B position and then push the lock with the private key into the C position, anyone with the public key can read the message by moving the lock back to the open B position. Although everyone has the public key, the private key is necessary first, so you can prove that you can turn the private key into a public key without making the private key public. This is how sending and receiving coins works with cryptocurrencies. If cryptocurrencies are obtained, these coins are encrypted using a public key (placed in a box). Anyone can do this because this key is publicly known. However, you can only send coins if you have the corresponding private key with which you can first open the box and then create a new transaction using the private key for signing. Since everyone has the public key, they can simply check the signatures of a private key for correctness and thus know for sure that someone really had the private key and was allowed to carry out the relevant transactions, i.e. blockchain updates. With other blockchain applications, such as contracts, everyone can read a contract with the public key, but only the person with the corresponding private key can edit it.

While there are a number of possibilities for generating private key - public key - pairs, such as prime factoring, elliptic curves are used for asymmetric key pair creation in the blockchain space. With Bitcoin, for example, this is $y^2 = x^3 + 7$. Starting from a point of origin, a certain number corresponding to the private key is mirrored on the curve until a number corresponding to the public key is reached. While the final result (public key) is very easy to calculate using the mathematical function, as long as you know the number of steps (private key), it is practically impossible to know how many steps were made (private key), if you only have the final result (public key). So, you always start with the number of mirroring steps(private key) and then you get the final result (public key), which you make public. Since these are enormously large numbers (for example 2^{256} possibilities for Bitcoin), it is practically impossible for two people or computers to generate the same private key.

If the cryptographic method of hashing is now combined with asymmetric key pairs, information can be created by anyone in a blockchain community and transformed into a combination of letters and numbers by hashing. This information can then only be processed by the person with the private key. Thereby, a blockchain remains open for everyone, but still contains simple rules, because with the creation and processing of information there is no interference.

In the workbook I have attached some documents, which go much further into detail:
www.morethanjustbitcoin.com

If you want to understand all these concepts in great detail, I can highly recommend to checkout my "crashcourse cryptography" on YouTube!

How do we now agree which information will be stored first in this digital file called a blockchain and which information will be stored afterwards if several updates take place at the same time?

CONSENSUS CREATION IN A BLOCKCHAIN (MINING)

> *Consensus creation in a decentralized system must by definition cost something to get all participants to store the best possible reality through an optimal consensus algorithm.*

With a blockchain there is no participant who is more or less important, but all participants are equal. Accordingly, everyone has the same right to enter information on the blockchain or have it entered. This applies as long as the cryptographic rules are adhered to and no changes are made that would not actually be allowed. But what happens if a participant first sends out an update, for example a „Yes", and shortly afterwards communicates the opposite information, for example a „No"? For consensus to be reached on a blockchain, at least 51 percent of the participants, i.e. the majority, must accept an entry on the blockchain. Only then is it considered „confirmed". If further blocks (updates) follow afterwards, this confirms the previous information, because in a blockchain a block can only be changed if all following blocks are also changed. From an economic point of view, it must therefore cost something to create a block, otherwise information can be created, changed or deleted free of charge. In addition, a free consensus creation could create numerous fake servers, which fictitiously represent 51 percent of the participants and thus could turn a decentralized system into a centralized system in the consensus voting, since these servers would not act independently in the end. This is called a Sybil attack. In order to avoid such a situation, a decentralized system requires fair consensus mechanisms.

The best-known consensus mechanism looks like this: In order to create a block (= an update), a participant must provide computing power with his computer with which a random hash must be recalculated to the original result. This hashing power is referred to as Proof of Work (PoW). This consensus mechanism is also known as mining and is the most famous among the public blockchains. The advantage is obvious: To perform an update on the blockchain, you have to prove that you have done some computing/calculation. This proof is very simple and can't be faked. You can theoretically do this calculation yourself and mine a block yourself. But in pretty much all blockchains you pay a Transaction Fee (or 'Tx-Fee') to a Miner, which takes care of that for you. The huge downside is that a lot of energy is spent on creating consensus. In some countries, such as Iceland for example, almost half of the country's total electricity consumption now goes into mining. Therefore, new, less wasteful consensus mechanisms are being feverishly worked on, as you will read in a moment.

Such fees for consensus creation can either be paid directly in the form of fees; they can also arise indirectly as costs, in that each computer does the work itself and pays the fee in this way. Fees can also be incurred in the form of inflation by giving Miners „free information" on the blockchain in addition to the Tx-fees when creating the consensus. This happens, for example, with cryptocurrencies in the form that coins are paid to miners via inflation. This is why many people mistakenly believe that mining a cryptocurrency is synonymous with coin creation. In reality, however, this is only a secondary function of mining and practically a consensus fee. With blockchains, which do not store financial information such as cryptocurrencies, a credit can also be given by mining beside the Tx-Fees, in order to be able to enter information afterwards free of charge, depending on which information is stored. If you take a look at cryptocurrencies, nothing else happens: The miner is given a value which is freely available for him afterwards. Other blockchain applications are simply about different information.

In addition to proof of work as a consensus mechanism, money can also be deposited and locked up as a type of cost. This is then called Proof of Stake (PoS). However, this mechanism is not yet very widespread due to some problems and is also quite controversial. There is also possibility of a fee as a „reputation risk". Such a proof-of-importance (PoI) model would theoretically be the best, since a good reputation is difficult to build up, but can easily be destroyed in the event of misconduct. Decentralized systems such as the Hashgraph are based on such a mechanism but have not yet been fully tested.

Compared to a centralized system, a decentralized system always entails higher costs. Furthermore, a decentralized system also has certain limits on the number of updates per second. Since each participant must be kept up-to-date with the current status of the file, a decentralized system on the basic structure is not infinitely scalable. Many blockchains here try to take shortcuts by centralizing their consensus. Instead of everyone participating in the consensus-building process, only a few of them do so. How meaningful this is for a pseudo-central system will only become apparent, however, when these few try to abuse the consensus.

Contradictory information (e.g. double spending with cryptocurrencies) can occur again and again, for example when an attacker tries to make a contract say one thing first and then another afterwards. In order to prevent this in a decentralized system, consensus is only regarded as given when information has been repeatedly confirmed. Since new information on the blockchain costs something, it becomes more and more expensive to try and change older information, since more and more new information also needs to be changed and the cost of that is getting higher with every new block. Of course, this only applies to a really decentralized system, because in a pseudo-central system you can manipulate information in a similar way to a centralized system.

If there are incompatible inconsistencies about the consensus in a blockchain, a fork occurs. The participants then assign themselves to one or the other group, depending on which information they regard as truth. Such forks can happen as „soft" forks (pure updates), or as „hard" forks if contrary information is stored on the respective information strands. In the long run, only very few hard forks are able to survive, as it is usually unprofitable at some point to continue the split consensus because of the costs. This brings us to the next point, which is how to create a blockchain.

HOW TO CREATE A BLOCKCHAIN?

> *Technically, you create a blockchain by defining the rules of the blockchain via the protocol and making them available to participants, who then keep the blockchain up to date.*

We will talk in one of the later chapters about the entrepreneurial activities in the blockchain space. The question of how to create a blockchain is more about a few technical ba-

sics. But I would like to point out two entrepreneurial questions to you right now:
1. Which information should be stored on the blockchain?
2. Why is a blockchain required for this solution?

The first question is easy to answer. The second question implies that you want to address a problem where the solution is an expensive, inefficient and slow system called blockchain. This sounds derogatory, but the costs for a decentralized system are higher than for a centralized system. In the entrepreneur chapter we will go into detail, because far too many entrepreneurs are not aware of these facts or only think too little and create a decentralized system, only because of the hype that comes with „blockchain".

Technically, one starts a blockchain with a whitepaper, in which the main features of the idea and its implementation are presented. The Ethereum whitepaper, which defines the current largest decentralized computer, can be found for example here: https://github.com/ethereum/wiki/wiki/White-Paper

The next step is to decide whether one wants to create a completely separate blockchain for one's undertaking, or whether this digital data can be stored by another, already existing blockchain whose underlying system you pay for. Today, most companies no longer start their own blockchains, but use other platforms as the basic structure. Bitcoin, currently the largest blockchain, makes this possible for example, via colored coins. The above-mentioned Ethereum does this via ERC20-Contracts (contracts based on the ERC20 standard), which also underpins the enormous value of both blockchains.

If you want to create your own blockchain, the next step is to clearly define the protocol for it. Here certain rules and procedures are fixed.

For instance: Which consensus algorithm is used? Is the blockchain „public" (publicly visible) or „private" (only visible to participants)? Is the blockchain permissioned or open for everyone? How are blockchain updates performed? The Bitcoin blockchain protocol, for example, can be found at the following link, which is regularly improved: https://en.bitcoin.it/wiki/Protocol_documentation

This results in different possibilities for decentralized systems:

- **Public & Open:** This is the gold standard, because anyone can join a blockchain and outsiders can view all updates on the ledger. Most large cryptocurrencies and decentralized computers are at this level.
- **Public & Permissioned:** Such a blockchain is publicly visible, but permissions are necessary in order to join it as a participant and to update it. Many of the logistics and transport blockchains are in this category.
- **Private & Open:** Such a blockchain is theoretically possible, but rarely used, because there are very few or no applications for it. To make something invisible from the outside, but at the same time to give every interested person access to it - usually doesn't make sense. Some decentralized data storage blockchains run like this or blockchains that want to identify the user (called KYC, „Know Your Customer", or KYB, „Know Your Business").
- **Private & Permissioned:** This blockchain is not visible from the outside and needs a permission to join it. Most corporate blockchains fall into this category.

Attention: If something is sold as „blockchain", but cannot be seen by the participants themselves, it is by definition a centralized system, because you cannot be sure if it is really decentralized. Many scams sell as Private & Permissioned but are nothing more than a centralized database with all its advantages and disadvantages. If the participants are told this openly, that's okay, but unfortunately many scams don't do that.

After these rules have been established, participants can join the blockchain and make updates.

HOW TO USE A BLOCKCHAIN?

> *Every private key already exists. The access to a blockchain is only created by choosing a private key from the almost infinite selection in order to then use the cryptography of a blockchain.*

Using a blockchain means nothing else than first saving the already existing information of the blockchain by means of the rules entered in the protocol and then interacting cryptographically with it. Because most people are not yet so familiar with decentralized systems, confusion often occurs here. . In centralized systems such as an online cloud system, you first register and then have access to the offered cloud storage. However, since a blockchain is decentralized, there is no database to which you can register. Random number generators are usually offered blockchain-specific but depending on the algorithm you could also use a specially designed one. In the area of cryptocurrencies, these random generators are called wallets.

Due to the mathematical formulas there are almost infinite possibilities for private keys. Thus it is practically impossible that ever in the history of the universe two people or machines generate the same private key. You can now derive the public key from this private key. If you want to receive data from another member, you have to send him your public key. As a sender, they encrypt the data with the public key, and only you can decrypt it yourself with the private key, which you must never give to anyone and must store securely. If you want to send data yourself, you sign the information with your own private key and can thus prove to each participant in the blockchain that you created this data yourself. This unique transaction is then permanently recorded on the blockchain. Regardless of whether the information is cryptocurrencies, digital contracts, logistics processes or other data - the use of blockchain always functions the same.

As already described in the chapter above, blockchains often differ in their use in terms of whether, for example, they are freely customizable and transparent for everyone or whether they have different characteristics. Public, freely accessible and completely transparent blockchains are the simplest, because anyone can use them, whether man or machine. You don't have to verify yourself and remain anonymous. All processes on the blockchain are transparent.

Using certain cryptographic methods such as ring signatures, mixers, zero-knowledge proofs, or even a new technology called Mimblewimble, a blockchain can be completely open and anonymous, but the processes on the blockchain are not transparent. Such blockchains offer increased privacy and could be used in the future, for example, in medicine and some other fields. With none of these blockchains you have to identify yourself during the private key generation, so you remain anonymous as a user.

Especially for blockchains like for example in the logistics area, where it is important to define processes and create transparency for all participants, algorithms can be created that force the participants to verify themselves in advance in order to use the blockchain afterwards.

Blockchains, which are used in-house for processes, cannot even be used from the outside. Here the blockchain can only be used within a defined group.

While each participant is theoretically equal, it has been shown that three groups usually form within a blockchain:

1. **Consensus creators:** They create consensus through various consensus mechanisms and receive fees from the users in return. For cryptocurrencies, the participants involved are called miners, master nodes or delegates.

2. **Users:** They use the blockchain and pay something to the consensus creators for updates. This fee does not always have to be paid directly, it can also happen indirectly via inflation or work.

3. **Full Nodes:** They ensure that all information is stored properly. They can, but don't have to be paid for it.

Important: With a true decentralized blockchain, it must be possible for each participant to exercise several or all roles at any time.

Many blockchains try to make compromises here, which goes hand in hand with a reduction in decentralization and thus stands in the way of the actual solution to the problem.

A possibility of increasing efficiency within a blockchain

through voluntary centralization is okay, but complete decentralization must be feasible at all times.

Therefore, the rules for the respective roles must also be presented openly; this is the only way to achieve independence from the solutions offered.

This does not mean that every user interface must be open source, but only that the underlying rules must be disclosed. Companies can thus not only build a user interface for a blockchain, but also market it economically.

However, a user need not fear that the underlying blockchain is gone when a company disappears that grants access to this blockchain. In this case, the user interface would be gone, but the information entered on the blockchain would ever be preserved.

Now that we have taken a closer look at a blockchain, we want to discuss the resulting advantages and disadvantages. We do this with the help of SWOT analysis.

SWOT ANALYSIS

SWOT analysis is a common method of analysis in which strengths, weaknesses, opportunities and threats are explored in terms of strategy, development or technical solutions. In the case of blockchain it also allows us to clearly analyze whether the hype surrounding this technology is justified or not. In addition, it allows conclusions to be drawn about the various possible applications and which potential alternatives could replace a blockchain. In the end, you always have to look at something from different angles in order to get as complete a picture as possible.

If you want to have all links and in-depth videos to this chapter, have a look at the regularly updated workbook which you either already got by e-mail or can get for free here: www.morethanjustbitcoin.com

THE SEVEN STRENGTHS OF BLOCKCHAIN TECHNOLOGY

The strengths of the blockchain also determine its weaknesses. The strengths of a blockchain can be divided into seven categories and are explained in the later chapters along with the seven large blockchain categories for the different application areas. Of course there are overlaps, but mostly a blockchain implementation mainly targets one of the areas and takes the other advantages along with it. The seven advantages of the blockchains have:

1. **Immutability**
2. **Privacy**
3. **Trust**
4. **Compatibility**
5. **Transparency**
6. **Redundancy**
7. **Inclusiveness**

Let's have a look on each point in detail now.

1. IMMUTABILITY

Every time data is entered on the blockchain, the community must come to a consensus and store the data independently on all servers involved. This creates the different consensus mechanisms (PoW, PoS, PoI etc.) costs. If you want to change the data afterwards, the same costs have to be spent again. After the information blocks of a blockchain are cryptographically linked via the merkle roots, one has to exchange not only the one block in which they are stored, but also all following blocks in order to change older data. The older the registered information is, the more expensive it is to exchange information afterwards. The larger the community is, the faster the point is reached that the cost of the change is far more expensive than the value of the newly entered information. It would therefore be an economic loss to change the blockchain retroactively. It does not make sense for any party to try this. For this reason, a blockchain is regarded as unchangeable, since entered information could only be changed at immense losses. For example, on the oldest blockchain, Bitcoin, data that was only a few hours old has never been changed. Changing information that is days, weeks or months old would quickly cost billions. In addition to cryptocurrencies, many other areas of application build on this advantage.

2. PRIVACY

A blockchain is based on cryptography, and so you can participate in data processing by creating a private key without further verification. This is in drastic contrast to most services offered on the Internet, where you have to register with your e-mail address or mobile phone number and thus reveal your identity. You can therefore act on a blockchain anonymously, which means that nobody knows who or what controls a private key. However, depending on whether the ledger (the update history) is readable, that is, transparent, or not, you can draw certain conclusions about the identity of a user through certain back calculations. Many blockchains are therefore called pseudo anonymous. Unfortunately, there is a lot of wrongly scattered information in the press about this, because it is often mistakenly claimed that blockchains favor illegal uses due to the increased privacy, but this is demonstrably not true. Quite the opposite: blockchains, due to their transparency, favor the documentation of possible crimes that would have otherwise not been verifiable.

3. TRUST

One of the most important strengths of a blockchain is its backbone consisting of mathematics and cryptography, which can be clearly calculated by anyone, regardless of culture, religion, race, history or belief structures. In almost no other field does the world agree on the facts as unambiguously as in mathematics. I have never met anyone who seriously believed that 1 + 1 would result in the number 3 or that the square root of 9 would be the number 4. The universal language of numbers is equally valid everywhere in the universe known to us so far and these open rules of a blockchain form the foundation stone for trust. Certainly, when people hear about it for the first time, everything is still unfamiliar, and it takes a little time for the stranger to become accustomed and familiar. Maybe you can remember your first online purchase for yourself. Entering the credit card number online certainly created a queasy feeling at first. But today, online shops like Amazon are an integral part of everyday life. It will be the same with trust in the blockchain algorithms.

4. COMPATIBILITY

One of the most powerful advantages of blockchain technology is to be interoperable. Blockchains can communicate with each other via protocols and exchange information without a middleman. For example, an identity blockchain can communicate freely with a real estate blockchain and automatically verify a buyer. Just as the Internet has broken down information barriers, blockchains will remove trust barriers step by step. This is also one reason why many governments, which would not need a blockchain for certain processes, are still researching this technology. This enables them to exchange information much more efficiently in their own system.

5. TRANSPARENCY

If a blockchain has been created with an algorithm that allows a transparent update overview, it allows full transparency. It is no longer necessary to trust the statement of a company or an audit company, but everyone can convince himself that what is claimed is true. Donations, elections, taxes, company audits and much more can be revolutionized by this advantage.

6. REDUNDANCY

Since a blockchain has to be decentralized by definition, there is immense redundancy in data storage. On the one hand this means inefficiency, on the other hand it means that it is impossible to destroy once created data. This means that certain programs, documents, contracts, etc. can be distributed all over the world and in the future all over the universe, thus providing excellent protection against practically any natural disaster. In order to create such redundancy, a system does not have to be completely decentralized. It is sufficient if the stored information is distributed far enough. A blockchain offers this advantage, but if the sole task is to create redundancy, a centralized, but widely distributed system would suffice. Here it is important to think carefully about which problem you want to solve and what the optimal solution should look like. We take a closer look at the details in the application chapter.

7. INCLUSIVENESS

A blockchain can be designed in such a way that everything and everyone can create a private key and join the community with it. This principle of not restricting access at all allows complete „inclusiveness", complete integration of all interested parties. If you look at the problems of many refugees or Third World countries, you can see that many centralized services follow an elitist principle. Those who are at the top of the food or distribution chain have it easier, those who are at the bottom have it harder to access it at all. A blockchain can help here. It knows no borders, no age, no status, no skin color, no religion, etc. By definition every participant of the blockchain is the same, because every person and every machine can generate a private key and participate in the cryptography. Of course, blockchains can also be „permissioned", i.e. a permission is required for participation, which is relevant within companies, for example. Nevertheless, many initiatives are being launched worldwide in the blockchain area, which use this openness as an advantage and therefore form the basis for many blockchain applications.

But everything has a flip side, and we will look at this in the next chapter.

THE SEVEN WEAKNESSES OF BLOCKCHAIN TECHNOLOGY

The weaknesses of blockchain technology mean you should only use a blockchain if it solves a problem better than a centralized system.

It is clear that a blockchain does not only have impressive advantages. Inevitably such a technology must also bring disadvantages with it, because the King of all Trades does not exist. Often these disadvantages are swept under the rug because blockchain followers are afraid that their „baby" (not a human being, but the still young and fragile technology) could not experience „growing up". But this is absolute nonsense. It merely leads to the formation of a fanboy community, as in a sect, in which rational thought is no longer given to the issue, but only blind chattering. This is not only a hindrance for blockchain development, but even dangerous, because just as you should tell your child that not everyone in the world is good, you have to be aware that blockchain is not suitable for every application. Otherwise you get involved in something wrong, which unfortunately happens far too often nowadays when blockchain solutions are designed for something for which no blockchain is needed. Many do not consider which core problem an application should solve, but rather what the own solution achieves, regardless of whether this makes sense or not. The main point is that the trend word 'blockchain' is in one's own solution.

The seven disadvantages of a blockchain are:

    1. Usability
    2. Costs
    3. Waste of resources
    4. Scaling limitation
    5. Rigidness
    6. Privacy
    7. Personal responsibility

Since I would like to talk about the different positive blockchain applications in the later chapters, I have kept the previous chapter on the advantages of a blockchain rather short as an overview - we are still often asked about the positive examples anyway.

On the other hand, I will make this chapter on the disadvantages a bit more detailed in order to really deal with a few „failures".

1. USABILITY

Even if everything sounds so great with this new technology at the beginning, one quickly realizes that (still) few functions are user-friendly. Since much is open source and not commercialized, companies focus more on the technical solution of a problem. However, this rarely contributes to user-friendliness. It is also extremely cumbersome for the customer to secure the private key in such a way that it cannot be burned or otherwise destroyed. The inheritance of information stored on the blockchain is also extremely difficult due to the decentralized system. If you have a problem, there is no customer support with a blockchain. Nobody is responsible, so there is no one you can turn to. So if you've ever wondered why big companies haven't jumped on the blockchain train despite the many advantages, it's partly because they're afraid that millions of people won't be able to log in irrevocably because they don't know their private key anymore.

Entrepreneurs, regulators and customers, however, are not allowed to throw the baby out with the bathwater. Just because not everything is working as it should in this field today, you don't have to write off the entire blockchain future right away. As expected, there will be a lot more to come in the area of user-friendliness. 20 years ago, the Internet was not yet suitable for the masses either, with a modem, a user interface that could not be operated intuitively and cumbersome steps. Blockchain technology is at a similar point today. Over time, this will improve through the use of clever entrepreneurs, just as it did with the Internet.

2. COSTS

In a centralized system, all participants trust the centralized party. The centralized party must devote more or less energy to maintaining this trust. In a decentralized system, a data entry must always cost something, because this is the only way to ensure that the information is unchangeable. If it were more profitable to change information stored on the blockchain, there would always come a time when a participant would take advantage of this. As already mentioned, the costs of a blockchain can arise in many ways. Either direct transaction fees or indirect costs such as inflation, work done, money deposited etc. are involved. If a decentralized system is to claim that no costs are necessary for the consensus, this can only mean the following: In reality, the system is not decentralized, but centralized, or the marketing does not give correct information, or the system is a rip-off, because it can easily be hacked.

It is precisely this cost point that is always misunderstood: People then mistakenly believe that a decentralized system would be cheaper than a centralized one. The opposite is the case. This makes it all the more important to ask oneself whether the inevitably increased costs of a decentralized solution are acceptable. Just because centralized systems have so far been able to charge fees for a service does not mean that they will continue to do so. In theory, a centralized system can reduce costs to almost zero. In a decentralized system this is not so easy, and the inevitable costs must be paid for. If they were at zero, the consensus could be changed again free of charge. This brings us to the next disadvantage, the waste of resources.

3. WASTE OF RESOURCES

In the chapter on consensus algorithms, we have discussed how the costs of consensus building come about. The most common principle is proof of work, in which everyone who wants to participate in the consensus has to solve a more or less pointless mathematical problem. As you might already have guessed, this process, also known as mining, is extremely wasteful. It is definitely not an environmentally friendly system to spend millions of USD every day on electricity to generate consensus. Countries like Iceland now consume more than half their electricity for mining. Other algorithms like Proof of Importance and Proof of Stake try to solve this, but these systems have inherent disadvantages compared to Proof of Work.

The fact that the ecological footprint is so bad due to traditional proof-of-work mining is one reason why environmentalists are right to criticize this and why many are pushing for consensus alternatives or at least for economically meaningful calculation tasks. In this way, attempts are made to create mathematical problems whose solution could result in real advantages in life. Such possibilities include DNA recombination calculations, prime number searches and much more. A few seem promising, but some hurdles on the way to full implementation have not yet been overcome. Even if the optimal solution does not yet exist, there is hope that this disadvantage of the blockchain will be significantly minimized in the future, even if it is still a rightly criticized point today. The next disadvantage of a blockchain is that everyone in the community needs to know about every update. This limits the possible number of updates and is called a scaling problem.

4. SCALING LIMITATION

Within a blockchain, each participant must have the same copy of the digital file for full consensus to prevail. This leads to a limit of possible updates per time unit, as each participant must have the technical ability to stay up to date. The limit is determined by the block size. If, for example, you know that an update is approximately 250 bytes, i.e. 0.25 kilobytes, in size and a block is to be a maximum of 1 megabyte, i.e. 1,000 kilobytes, in size, a maximum of approximately 4000 updates per block and time unit can be performed in this case.

If you want to achieve a higher scaling on the blockchain itself, you have to reduce the update size. However, this is only possible to a certain extent, because information needs at least a bit of data memory. Alternatively, you can increase the possible storage capacity, i.e. the block size. However, this causes an increased amount of data. In this case each participant would not only need more storage space, but also a higher transmission speed. In order to remain really decentralized and inclusive, one must orient oneself to the weakest link in the chain and take the slowest and weakest standard. Otherwise one creates an oligarchy in which only a few participants with well-equipped computers can fully participate in the consensus.

Some blockchains try to compromise here to overcome this disadvantage. They reduce decentralization by tightening the conditions for consensus. So no longer do everyone participate in the consensus, but only a few selected participants. Personally, I am very skeptical about this, because it leads past the original problem, for the solution of which a blockchain was actually created. If you want efficiency, you only need a centralized system. A system that is not 100 percent decentralized is abused at the wrong moment by the controlling party. Therefore, I believe that such pseudo-central blockchains are created only for the hypes and not for the sake of the actual solution.

Even if there is no perfect scaling solution today, I personally consider the off-chain or 2nd layer options to be the most promising. Here the basic layer is managed as a completely decentralized blockchain with all the advantages and disadvantages. Then participants of the blockchain can join together to a 2nd layer (a second level) and create a partial consensus based on the blockchain. You don't need to inform everyone else in the group about the updates unless these updates affect people outside the group. We will discuss these solutions in detail in a later chapter. The only thing that is important for understanding is that it is essential for a blockchain that the base layer is completely decentralized and thus resistant to censorship. So you always have a safety net and don't have to rely on other systems. If, on the other hand, you want to build a basic structure with centralization, you quickly bring the disadvantages of centralization into the system, and the whole construct collapses. This also becomes exciting when we look at possible blockchain alternatives such as the tangle or the hash graph at the end of the book.

5. RIGIDNESS

The only thing that never changes is the change itself. Based on this credo, another weak point of a blockchain comes to light: It's incredibly difficult to integrate upgrades because it requires the approval of the majority of the community. However, as we know, there are as many different opinions as there are participants about what something should be like. The fact that blockchains cannot be taken over by one party is on the one hand a huge advantage, on the other hand it leads to a rigidness, which in the long run can make a once successful blockchain obsolete.

If a blockchain community does not agree on a consensus, it splits into different forks. Such forks either happen intentionally because a part of the community wants to split off, or unintentionally because one cannot agree on a sustainable consensus. Forks have a common history of consensus, but then they no longer agree at a certain point in time. If you look at most of the large blockchains today, you can see from the numerous forks how often such unresolved discrepancies occur. In order to avoid the rigidness of a blockchain and the emergence of new forks, many agree on the necessity of so-called smart rules. These are smart rules that regulate the future of the blockchain either with or without the participation of the community. Some smart rules already exist, such as the Mining Difficulty. This is the mathematic difficulty to be successful in the proof-of-work consensus. The more participants take part in mining, the more difficult it is to find a solution for the mathematical problem that has to be solved in order to complete a block. Through this regulation, the speed is distributed over the entire group and remains fairly constant over time. Since this default is a preset algorithm, it corresponds to a smart rule. Smart rules could also be integrated for new upgrades or new features - algorithms that are only just beginning to be used for blockchains today. Such integrated smart rules will, however, be necessary in a large area, otherwise a once successful blockchain will be replaced by a newer, better one as quickly as the former „dumb phones" by smartphones.

6. PRIVACY

The penultimate disadvantage may surprise you a little, since privacy was already listed among the benefits. You may now think that I am referring to the possible illegal use of blockchains by the anonymity of users, as the press often describes it. However, this is largely incorrect, since many studies clearly prove that blockchains are used for considerably more legal applications than is the case with non-blockchain applications. No, this disadvantage concerns the lack of privacy due to the use of a blockchain due to its high transparency.

Since with a blockchain in most cases it is comprehensible for eternity which updates have been carried out, one can become a transparent person through their use. Of course this is not desirable, because nobody will want, for example, his insurances to be public or everyone to know which investments he or she owns. As already mentioned before, there are solutions in which the user behavior is masked by additional cryptographic methods, but then everything is masked. A mix in which a certain part of the information is masked, and another part is not would be optimal. Teams are currently working on such possibilities, which can largely eliminate this disadvantage.

7. PERSONAL RESPONSIBILITY

The last disadvantage is the reason why so many people find it so difficult to use a blockchain: Since no one is in charge, everyone is responsible for themselves. Even if many people believe that they would like to have more personal responsibility, it becomes apparent again and again that the majority of people prefer to pass it on to someone else. This explains why so many people are not interested in their finances or their health. In the end, they prefer to give the responsibility for it to other people - unfortunately often without success. In a centralized system, a party clearly has control, and therefore responsibility lies with it. This is lacking in a decentralized system. Even though I like to see myself as responsible, every time I stay at a hotel I am grateful that I can get a new room key card at the reception if I have lost the original one. Of course, this only works because the hotel has a centralized room management. A little funny anecdote is a video about a poor hotel guest who has to experience this for himself. You can watch it under the following link: https://www.youtube.com/watch?v=Qnxq-1Qmg5Y

Facebook could theoretically also have a decentralized account management where you log in with a private key and then create your own profile as a public key. However, I suspect that over time almost all users would lose their private key and thus access to their account at some point and would therefore no longer be able to use Facebook. Facebook would lose its business model of data usage as a result. If you have ever had to request your password from a service, remember that this only works because the system is centralized, and your password is stored in encrypted form in a database.

Even if I want to help here with my #CRYPTOFIT movement, it probably won't work completely decentralized. People need customer support and want to held by the hand with certain things. Exactly why I also believe that in the future a mix of decentralized and centralized will prevail. This is similar to how nobody wants a pure anarchy or monarchy, even if both would theoretically work on paper - as long as everything runs perfectly. Problems always arise when something doesn't work perfectly and needs to be helped out. So we prefer something in the middle between monarchy and anarchy, and a similar development will take place in the questions of centralization or decentralization. However, it will be crucial that these systems complement each other and that they do not mix at the same time. So it must not be a system of 60 percent decentralization and 40 percent centralization, but a 100 percent decentralized system must work together with a 100 percent centralized system, with each system eliminating the disadvantages of the other.

If we now come to the different blockchain applications (opportunities of the SWOT analysis), we will address these questions in detail and also work out possible solution models. We divide the applications according to the seven different advantages, and it will again be important to remember that an application only has a right to exist if a real problem is solved by decentralization. As you will see, this is unfortunately not always the case.

BLOCKCHAIN APPLICATION 1: OWNERSHIP

Due to the immutability of a blockchain it is perfectly suited to display ownership uncensurable and irrevocable. We now start into the application chapters, where I will tell you about 100 fields, which are revolutionized by blockchain in the sense of a disruptive (i.e., displacing the old) technology. The areas are sorted according to the main advantage that the use of a blockchain brings them. Of course, there is no case where an area uses only one single advantage, and so I combine the individual fields into almost 50 groups and also address the other advantages through cross-referencing. Each of the following seven chapters begins with a reminder of the advantage on which the respective group is based. This is also the case in this chapter - the chapter about the application of ownership.

When I discuss the different applications, I always follow the same procedure, which seems sensible from an entrepreneurial point of view, in order to make it easier for you to get started in a particular field:

1. **Problem description:** The problem, which should be solved by a blockchain in any given field, should always be stipulated at the beginning of a chapter. Remember, a blockchain solution without a real usecase will fail.

2. **Solution explanation:** Here I describe the blockchain application, which (hopefully) corresponds to an optimal solution.

3. **Challenges:** Very few solutions have already been implemented - quite the opposite. They all struggle because of some challenges, which often have nothing to do with blockchain directly. I list them here, because it often takes people outside the community who might have a good idea to help the blockchain solution to break through. In order for online shops, for example to have become successful, good logistics providers were needed for fast deliveries of goods.

4. **Alternative possibilities:** Is blockchain the only solution to solve the problem discussed, or are there others? This is not so much a question of alternative, decentralized solutions, but rather of investigating the necessity of a blockchain. Sometimes no blockchain is necessary to solve the problem, but companies only start a blockchain for the hype's sake.

5. **Practical examples:** The point here is not to list individual projects, but rather to show a few relevant examples from practice. Since the blockchain domain is generally still very young and it is very difficult to know at such an early stage which blockchain solution will be successful and which will not, I will not explicitly mention project names in order to remain as neutral as possible.

In addition to the application chapters, you will also find a short general entrepreneurs' chapter for the blockchain area to inform you about questions such as employee recruitment, finance and general strategies. So let's start with the first blockchain application in the „Ownership" category.

CRYPTOCURRENCIES (FINANCIAL SECTOR)

Problem description: Even if this book should contain as little as possible about cryptocurrencies, they have to be mentioned first as the currently largest area of application of a blockchain. Nevertheless I will keep this chapter relatively short. If you're more interested in this topic here, you can get an explanation of cryptocurrencies, which has sold over 100,000 times in over ten languages: www.cryptofit.community

If you ask people which problem cryptocurrencies like Bitcoin should solve, you get the most different answers, for example: protection against inflation! Immediate transactions! Cheaper payments! Unfortunately, the fewest answers are correct. For example, many cryptocurrencies are rare in themselves, but they can be copied at will. Furthermore, the transaction speeds in decentralized systems are generally slower than in centralized systems, and the costs are higher and not lower. Exactly these misunderstandings lead to the fact that the mass of people, cheered on by the media, are uncertain whether cryptocurrencies actually solve a problem or not. What problem do cryptocurrencies solve now? If you look at them today rather as digital gold, they solve the problem of hedging: a state cannot simply take a decentralized currency away from its owner. Gold on the one hand, can be taken away to a certain extent; Crypto coins controlled by a private key, on the other hand, cannot really be expropriated. So if one tries to solve the problem of universal protection against the centralized financial world, one cannot avoid rare „digital gold". This corresponds to cryptocurrencies. From my point of view, this usecase is most likely to apply today. The currency aspect is more likely to develop in the future.

Solution explanation: With cryptocurrencies, the account balances of the participants are not controlled centralized by a bank or a state, but decentralized by the community via a blockchain. The reason why this application was the first to establish itself in 2009 is that money is relatively easy to display and use digitally. The first cryptocurrency called Bitcoin was defined by an unknown inventor with the pseudonym Satoshi Nakamoto in a whitepaper in 2008 and actively launched in early 2009. Since then, the value of a bitcoin has increased thousands of times, which has largely led to the crypto hype of the last years. Cryptocurrencies hold the promise to be usable by everyone, not controllable or censurable and extremely fast. They should also be able to prevent hyperinflation. Since the early years there have been thousands of cryptocurrencies, and the press either celebrates or insults them. The reason for this, besides the volatile price development, is the unclear question for which problem cryptocurrencies have been created exactly as a solution.

Challenges: The biggest challenge which cryptocurrencies have to master is that of marketing. I don't mean that many people believe that cryptocurrencies are mainly used for illegal purposes, which is demonstrably not true. Rather, I mean that people today see cryptocurrencies more as an „insurance against the financial world" and not (yet) so much as currency. This is called crypto asset and not cryptocurrency. With the right understanding, the acceptance and thus the use itself will come later. Another challenge is that of regulation. It is difficult to regulate decentralized currencies, but exchanges can very well be regulated. One of the reasons why I am part of the blockchain initiatives of the European Union is precisely this one. It is advisable for companies to work closely with the regulator in order to clear up misunderstandings and make the best possible use of regulatory opportunities.

If you are wondering when cryptocurrencies will be usable as currency, it will certainly take some time.

Alternative possibilities: That cryptocurrencies will assert themselves as „asset worth", i.e. as crypto assets, is very probable or has already happened. There is no real alternative here, as it is by definition an insurance against the centralized managed Fiat money system. It remains to be seen, however, whether cryptocurrencies can assert themselves as true currencies. There are simply enough alternatives, which do not have to be perfect. They only have to be good enough, especially if they already serve the main purpose. It is the inertia of an existing network that makes it so difficult to install new networks. Centralized managed currencies can react agilely to economic changes due to interest rates - or, of course, destroy much through hyperinflation. Nevertheless, it will be difficult for cryptocurrencies to completely replace fiat currencies. The fact that countries are fundamentally opposed to cryptocurrencies is a myth that persists. Banks and states are in principle open to cryptocurrencies, but nobody knows yet what the perfect cryptocurrency looks like. Everyone is waiting, while only one person is needed to get things moving. This will happen. Because just as only a good centralized currency is needed to give decentralized currencies almost no chance, a widely accepted decentralized currency is enough to declare war on the centralized currencies.

Apart from the centralized currencies, all decentralized currencies are of course in strong competition with each other. Meanwhile there are thousands of cryptocurrencies, which all want to claim the status of „digital gold" for themselves. How many are really necessary remains to be seen, however. I guess, just a few handful. So prepare yourself for the fact that 99 percent of all already existing cryptocurrencies will disappear. A cryptocurrency is rare in itself, but not in the totality of the cryptocurrencies, because you can always copy them. This remains a risk factor that must be considered when asking whether there are possible alternatives to the current solution.

Practical examples: Because it is so easy to create a cryptocurrency, there are now thousands of variations, some of which are permission free and transparent, others permissioned and not transparent. Some have a constant inflation built in, others are quantitatively limited to a maximum (a „cap") and therefore deflationary. Some cryptocurrencies have rigid rules, others have smart rules, and some have even a development fund that pays the developers of the crypto currency. Whether you should invest in cryptocurrencies or not is easy to answer: a clear „yes". The problem is only in which of the thousands an investment is worthwhile. Personally I would classify it as highly probable that one of the cryptocurrencies in question will become dominant, but nobody knows which one it will be. Therefore, every investment in the crypto sector must be classified as a high-risk investment.

Cryptocurrencies will massively revolutionize the financial sector:

- Banks will have to consider how to gain even more trust from customers through decentralized systems.
- Now that transaction fees worldwide will be close to zero, companies like Western Union will have to consider other revenue models.
- Money changers will also struggle, as currencies that can be used globally will make remittance less important.
- Online payment service providers like PayPal have to rethink. Instead of gaining complete control over customers' money, they must offer a service with interfaces rather than a complete solution for processing payments.

- In the future, customers will really want to own their money themselves and this can only be done with a blockchain.

If innovative financial institutions want to already make first attempts in this area, then a service could offer its customers decentralized ownership of money, while certain features such as the user interface remain centralized. Whoever believes that the financial model of the last 100 years will continue for another 100 years will only have to look at all those areas that have been completely revolutionized by the Internet. Blockchain will turn the question of a provider's trustworthiness upside down, and banks have benefited greatly from the trust their customers have placed in them. However, if trust can be created differently, then profit is also made differently. So I can only advise every actor in the financial sector to think through these consequences in detail and to let blockchain flow into their own business model.

Now the topic of cryptocurrencies is closed, and we can devote ourselves to the other, sometimes much more exciting blockchain discussions.

MILES AND POINTS (LOYALTY PROGRAMS, CREDIT CARDS, AIRLINES)

Problem description: Many people are familiar with Miles & More, the largest mileage collection program of European airlines. Payback, credit card points and other loyalty programs all work in a similar way. These mileage programs or accrual points work almost like a currency, except that they are issued and used internally by a company or a merger. The programs are designed to increase customer loyalty to their own company. Therefore, each company uses its own program. Some of the points of cryptocurrencies apply here as well, but there are other challenges.

In the course of a consulting assignment at one of the largest banks in Europe, the topic of loyalty programs came up for discussion. When I was asked what the bank needed, I was answered: the greatest wish of most people who participate in a loyalty program is to have more points of acceptance for the points collected and not need thousands of different programs. But a loyalty program is not meant to give up all power, nor to make everything completely transparent. In addition, those responsible would not have the time to worry about acceptance points all over the world. So how do we solve these problems?

Solution explanation: Miles and points are normally stored in a centralized database and can be inflated (created) unlimited. For outsiders, such systems are completely intransparent. At the same time, they are completely isolated from other programs, which leads to the problems described above. In order to give a company more control over the program, but to allow the customer more transparency and interaction with their programs, a mix could be created: On the one hand a centralized database, in which the customer's points are created and which cannot be viewed from the outside, and on the other hand an exchange option, in which points are changed from the database to a public blockchain. This so-called peg can work in both directions or only in one. There can also be an exchange rate. This is essential, because on a blockchain suddenly completely different possibilities for customers arise than in a centralized database. Points are now interchangeable with other coins and can be used practically ubiquitously, while the company still controls the main parts of its system.

Bringing a loyalty program onto the blockchain creates an additional advantage if others do the same, thus creating interoperability. Of course, a loyalty program can be linked to a cryptocurrency. However, it becomes really exciting when many loyalty programs join together in this way to form a metaprogram. Unlike many other applications, loyalty programs require little communication with the physical world, so there is no friction here. But just a new area, which is based on a network character, needs other parties.

This leads to some challenges.

Challenges: it is a chicken-and-egg problem where everyone is waiting for the other. This is the case with many technical innovations. Another challenge arises from the partial transparency of the program and the associated consequences. Customers may be surprised at how many points there actually are, and regulators may demand additional financial reserves to guarantee the redemption of the points. Whether the providers of loyalty programs want this or not is up to them alone. Nevertheless, it is possible to use blockchains to solve the problem described above - something I have not only said to the bank in my consulting speech, but rather emphasized: Because of the advantages, it will be a must to make your own loyalty program open.

Alternative possibilities: Of course, loyalty programs could also merge. Payback, Miles & More and many credit card programs are already trying to do this. In addition, points could be displayed more transparently for customers. This would be a clear alternative and would make a blockchain inefficient. It remains to be seen which implementation will finally prevail. But the past shows that open systems are usually easier to implement than closed and strongly controlled systems.

Practical examples: Banks, credit card companies, airlines, hotels, car rental companies and even companies like Grab should pay attention here if they consider bringing their loyalty program onto a blockchain, in order to keep it attractive. Especially because it is very easy to setup a first usecase as a token on another blockchain without much cost or knowledge.

GAMING TOKEN (COMPUTER GAMES)

Problem description: Gaming tokens are similar to a currency in a computer game, which is a closed system. These tokens can be exchanged for special features in the game. For example you can buy a special sword, buy special costumes for the character or change them into other so-called skins. Gaming tokens can be bought either with regular money, by exchanging them with other players or by achieving certain goals in the game. Gaming tokens are controlled by the gaming company via a centralized database, and every centralized system needs the trust of the community, in this case the other players. Many of the digital skins or weapons in a game that can be bought have value because the game manufacturer promises to keep them rare. For example, the big golden sword only exists once in a game. But how can a player be sure that this is the case?

Solution explanation: The possession of tokens or skins could easily be displayed transparently via a blockchain. Similar to loyalty programs, the gaming tokens could also be made more compatible with other programs via a blockchain, and so the problems of many gaming tokens would be solved quite simply.

Challenges: The big challenge with this application is that there are only a few providers of computer games that dominate the entire field. In principle, there are perhaps five to ten companies that dominate the entire computer game market.[14] Even though competition between the individual parties is high, interoperability is not quite as essential as, for example, with loyalty programs, of which there are thousands. It is therefore not in the absolute interest of the big players to create many advantages for customers here, and an outside company will find it difficult to sell its blockchain solution to one of the computer game companies.

Alternative possibilities: As long as a computer game company doesn't cheat the players, gaming tokens don't inflate indefinitely, and skins are rare, the call for a decentralized but clearly less efficient solution won't get loud too quickly. Interoperability or transparency can also be created, albeit only to a limited extent, by centralized solutions. The gaming token solution may seem interesting, but the exact

---

14 https://www.zippia.com/advice/biggest-video-game-companies-in-america/

implementation will take some time.

Practical examples: Vitalik Buterin, one of the founders of the Ethereum blockchain, was quoted that he „happily played World of Warcraft from 2007 to 2010, until the Blizzard company changed a destructive component of his character. He cried himself to sleep and knew that centralization was horror".[15] Whether it really happened that way or not is not important at all. At the same time, this humorous statement clearly illustrates the power decentralization would have in a computer game: The player would really be in possession and thus in control of the digital things he bought in the game.

In 2017, the collection game Cryptokitties was introduced on the Ethereum blockchain, where you can collect digital cats. I considered this to be one of the most important blockchain developments in that year. For the first time people could really own this digital asset of a game and didn't need to rely on other companies. Cryptokitties is not a really relevant blockchain application. But it was the first time that a player could still own his cats, even if the company went bankrupt. It would also be comparable with special weapons or costumes when using a blockchain in the field of computer games. If a game went broke, they could become even more valuable due to their rarity.

---

15 https://about.me/vitalik_buterin

Should large computer game manufacturers decide to decentralize tokens and skins, this would have an enormous impact on the other manufacturers. Depending on the success of the implementation, transparency and interoperability would be possible to a completely different extent than before. Whether and when this will happen, however, remains to be seen.

MEDIA CONTENT (INSTAGRAM, YOUTUBE ...)

Problem description: Digital content like photos or videos surround us every day on the net. We can upload, copy or delete them on numerous platforms. However, once these digital contents are put online, it quickly becomes quite difficult to know to whom the photo or video in question originally belonged to. Is it still the original photo, or has it been changed? So, how could one document the possession of such digital content without having to trust anyone?

Solution explanation: Instead of trusting a centralized company which documents the ownership, this could simply be presented in a trustless decentralized manner via a blockchain. If a photo or video is uploaded, the property is registered on a blockchain and thus documented. If the platform itself would then close, the uploaded files would not simply be gone. The user really owns the data himself. Additionally the photo or video can be coded by a hash in such a way that a change of the original file would lead to a changed hash. If you want to prove the ownership, you can, similar to cryptocurrencies, simply sign something and prove the original ownership with the same private key with which the photo was created.

Challenges: The big challenge with this blockchain application is the numerous possibilities of how and where we upload digital things to the net. So it would need a blockchain standard that holds all possessions. Whether the big players like Facebook, Google etc. allow this will be an essential question that will decide on the potential success of such an application. It is conceivable that such a blockchain would start in at least one niche. Scaling, on the other hand, definitely needs a lot of political and economic power. Just because companies promise such an application does not mean that it will become widespread.

Alternatives: Either such a system is not started at all, or one of the big players in the digital field creates a centralized database in which the hashes of the digital files are stored as proof of ownership. If, for example, you upload a photo to Instagram, you get a unique hash which can be combined with a time stamp and thus represents proof of ownership. This would then be a centralized alternative solution for this problem.

Practical examples: Whether it is decentralized or centralized will always depend on trust in the company. If our data is misused, the call for decentralized, but not so efficient solutions quickly becomes loud. In one of the next chapters, we will once again talk about privacy, which can be created by a blockchain. Whether and to what extent photos, videos or other digital files are stored on the Internet will depend not only on one factor, but on many others. Every company that offers digital storage, however, should take a close look at the different possibilities when it comes to representing digital ownership via a blockchain. By that I mean by far not only Instagram and YouTube.

DOCUMENTS (PDFS, NOTARIAL DEEDS OR CONTRACTS ...)

Problem description: At first glance you might think that documents on a blockchain have a similar purpose as photos or videos: It's mainly about the proof of its original owner. This may partly be the case with e-books. But an even more important problem is here the clear documentation of a document or its versions during the creation process. If you want to keep an agreement about a Word file and make sure that nobody changes anything afterwards, there is practically no way around a PDF file. Otherwise you can easily turn a „1,000" into a „10,000". DocuSign, for example, secures digital contracts online. How, however, can a document be saved unchanged without a centralized party, so that it is also ensured that the content is exactly the same as before when it is called up again?

Solution explanation: With a blockchain this is easily possible. The document is hashed and given a unique Hash-ID. This is stored on the blockchain and ensures that other document versions are clearly recognizable by another ID. Even different document versions with time stamps could be used differently, and everyone could sign such a document with their own private key. If people are extremely suspicious of the state and are afraid that it might smuggle in incriminating documents onto their computer, it would even be possible to hash an entire hard disk. If something is changed during an external access to the hard disk, one can inevitably prove what the hard disk looked like before. It remains to be seen to what extent this will one day be a use case for blockchains. .

Challenges: They are similar to those of the blockchain for photo and video files. Apart from a missing standard, the necessary storage space is still required. This is not only necessary to document the original, but also to save it in its original state. Otherwise you have a unique hash on the blockchain, but when the original file is gone, you only know that an existing file is not the same file as the one that created the hash. But then the content of the original is not known. We will talk about the advantages and disadvantages of decentralized data storage. However, this is currently an unsolved problem, which should hopefully be improved by better storage and transfer possibilities.

Alternative possibilities: Centralized alternatives like DocuSign already exist. Until decentralized versions become established, the correct standard must be defined for this and storage options must be found.

Practical examples: There are already first tests in which documents are hashed and then the seed is saved on the blockchain. Due to the relatively low costs this can be done with important documents even with every new document version. Here, however, you have to save the files yourself, and only the hash is decentralized. Should such Proof of Concepts prevail, this would pave the way for larger projects. This would then have severe effects on notaries and all other companies in the offline and online sector, which store contracts for customers in a centralized manner as trusted partners.

REGISTRY (LANDS, PROPERTIES, REAL ESTATE …)

Problem description: For centuries, or perhaps even millennia, the ownership of land and property has been one of the most important symbols of prosperity and status. For many people it is a dream to own their own piece of land with a cottage on it. Although such ownership information is recorded in a land registry in most industrialized countries, there are many more countries where such an entry is no guarantee of real ownership. Even if expropriations are a thing of the past in Europe or North America, they are still the order of the day in some countries of South America, Africa and Asia. This unsettles the own population and leads to riots. Uncertainty about possessions also prevents foreign companies from making necessary investments in a country. There is a lack of predictability as to whether a government, in spite of a corresponding entry in the land registry, will not simply go ahead, declare it null and void and expropriate the land, property or real estate there.

Solution explanation: A blockchain could help here. Instead of registering the ownership of land only in a centralized registry, each landowner, for example, also stores the land ownership of each other. The costs for this blockchain could be borne by a small tax on the property. This would at the same time secure the decentralization of the blockchain. In order not to lose a private key, for example, certain steps could, depending on the regulation, only be taken with permissions from authorities. In this way, one could somehow get one's private key back after losing it; however, no centralized party can change anything without permission that is represented in this decentralized system.

Challenges: The challenges of this solution are often emotional in nature. On the one hand, nothing is more important to people than their own home. They want to make sure that nobody can take it away from them and for that reason they would love the concept of a blockchain. On the other hand, however, some people find it weird when their own possessions are suddenly no longer readable in a land registry but are distributed over numerous computers. I still remember a heated discussion with my father, in which he jumped up from the dining table in rage, because he could not imagine that plots of land would ever not be stored in a centralized registry. Just as this may still be unimaginable for him today, it will take a while for many people to get to grips with the idea. The solution here is to initially operate two systems in parallel, a centralized registry and a property blockchain - the latter probably on a voluntary basis at the beginning. After some time, perhaps years or even decades, there will be complete trust in the decentralized system. Then the land registry can be omitted. This can be compared with dictionaries whose online version was initially regarded as an addition to physical dictionaries, but which are now generally used as the main reference.

Alternative possibilities: Of course, there must be benefits for all parties - not just the landowners. The state must also profit, otherwise it will not simply hand over the power of property control. If a state wants to gain the trust of foreign partners, predictability must exist. This is essential for developing countries in particular. Of course, this does not necessarily require the creation of a blockchain, but this could help enormously. As always, the centralized system, which enjoys general trust, is a top alternative - as long as this existing trust is not abused. On the other hand, a distributed solution could also be created instead of a decentralized one. Here a centralized party can decide on the entries, but numerous copies of the entry registry remain with the participants. In the event of misuse based on the documentation, they can file charges in a simpler manner. Especially in such an application, speed and scaling make a decentralized system possible. In many other applications, such as currencies, update limits often inhibit breakthroughs. In usecases such as land registries, where an update is not carried out every millisecond this is unlikely to be as important.

Practical examples: Fortunately, many countries worldwide are doing research in this direction. A few years ago, for example, I was in India for a consulting project in this area. In an investment pitch in 2015, we won a sum of USD 15,000 for such a project in Africa; and countries in South America or the US states are also testing different possibilities in this application category. An additional advantage of a blockchain solution is the blockchain interoperability, which we will discuss later. This interoperability allows an easier exchange of values on a blockchain. In theory, gold, loyalty points and much more could be exchanged directly into real estate without the additional costs and transaction speeds of currencies.

IDENTITY (NATIONALITY, PASSPORTS, IDENTITY CARDS ...)

Problem description: People have been identifying themselves for centuries by means of identity cards. Regardless of whether proof of Reich membership in the Middle Ages or passports today - these identification documents issued by a centralized authority prove who we are and where we come from. Whether we are talking about identification theft, which has become one of the most common thefts of all, or the problem of having no ID document at all, either because it was lost, stolen or no longer recognized due to political problems - proving one's own identity is a daily challenge that surrounds us. What if someone has a copy of your passport and uses it to create fake profiles on the Internet? What if a country goes to war and its inhabitants become political refugees without valid documents? Many of these problems could be prevented if identification were decentralized rather than centralized.

Solution explanation: With an identification blockchain, the participants could unambiguously verify other participants. Instead of a passport, you would have a unique public key, which would gain verification and reputation through interaction with others on the blockchain. For example, a state would have a key for a proof of state and would sign your public key. The hospital could do the same to create the birth certificate. In the end, a digital identity is created that is anonymous online, but can be clearly assigned to the person concerned via a key. One would no longer need to show a passport or enter its data for an identification but could simply sign something with one's identity. This could prove who you are, and nobody could go here and sign something else with someone else's identity. The numbers of identity thefts would decrease noticeably. In addition, it would be much more difficult to create fake identities. Because instead of forging a passport, you would have to create different keys out of nothing, including the corresponding time stamps. Because time stamps, i.e. the indication when something happened, cannot be faked on a blockchain, one would have to wait 25 years, for example, until a 50-year-old, who would have to look like a 25-year-old, could use a fake ID card. Any change would be clearly visible, and processes that make no sense would not be recognized by another party. At the same time, such an identity would be difficult to deprive someone of. It would be like trying to steal someone's bitcoins. Of course, that is possible, but it is much harder than simply blocking someone's passport or taking it away. Political refugees would still be able to identify themselves, and the passport of Edward Snowden, for example, could never have been invalidated.

Challenges: Of course, there are even more challenges to overcome for identification on the blockchain than there are already partial solutions. On the one hand, it must be clarified how the private key is stored. The risk of having created it and then losing it is far too high. The best possibility would be to create the private key from biological features, for example by taking the fingerprint, iris scan or facial features. Unfortunately, these are partly easy to forge. Therefore, in my personal opinion, this blockchain solution only becomes suitable for mass production when our brain can interact directly with a computer. This will probably not be the case in the distant future. This conclusion is obvious if you look at the technical possibilities around bionic prostheses, in which patients can move artificial joints by their thoughts alone. In the future, we will probably create our own private key for the unambiguous identification by our own brain. In addition to this problem of human-blockchain interaction, which by the way will still be a frequently mentioned problem of many blockchain solutions, there is of course the problem of trust in such a system. Suddenly you no longer have a passport in your hand but have to trust that all other nodes in the network confirm that you are who you seem to be pretending to be. Furthermore, such a solution does not have to be decentralized.

Alternative possibilities: Theoretically, such an identification solution could also be implemented via a centralized system. Facebook, for example, could generate a kind of ID document, which is already being used in part for online verification. Mergers of states would also have the possibility of storing the ID documents of their citizens centrally, but still distributed, and thus improving the possibilities of identification.

Practical examples: There are already many attempts in this direction - both positive and negative in nature. In South Africa, for example, the first beer vending machine was presented that checks decentrally whether you are older than 21 years and thus whether you meet the legal requirements to get a beer.[17] Of course, these examples are nothing more than a proof of concept and should rather be seen as a gag. But large-scale government projects are already in their infancy. The call for too much transparency and absolute control by Big Brother must not be forgotten. In China, for example, there are first attempts to get complete control over the citizens through such an identity and thus to achieve a division of society according to their wellbeing.[18] As already

---

17 https://www.coindesk.com/the-worlds-first-crypto-beer-vending-machine-has-arrived/
18 https://en.wikipedia.org/wiki/Social_Credit_System

mentioned with the strengths and weaknesses of decentralized systems, such things must in any case be considered in the first place.

PATENTS AND TRADEMARKS (PATENT OFFICE, IP ASSOCIATIONS ...)

Problem description: Anyone who has ever wanted to establish a company, register a trademark or secure an invention has already been faced with the same question: When should I register a trademark or a patent? How expensive is a registration? Where do I have to register the trademark or patent? Is there already a registration of another person at the patent office? Unfortunately, it is not easy to answer all these questions, because patent applications are regulated differently in every country worldwide, and there are numerous different associations. Registrations are expensive and (patent) attorney searches are time-consuming.

Solution explanation: For the reasons mentioned above, patents are a prime example of a blockchain. If you combine timestamps with a hash starting from a patent content, you get a blockchain which defines the exact time of a patent application and the exact content of the patent. In addition, this blockchain is completely transparent and accessible to everyone. Hash collisions would be partially recognizable as already existing patents and would reduce (patent) attorney costs. Patent ownership would thus be clearly defined both in terms of time and ownership and would be available at lower costs than today's complex solutions.

Challenges: Apart from the fact that associations worldwide would have to agree on a blockchain standard for patents, there is still the challenge of how to convert different patents into hashes uniformly. However, these are problems that many other blockchain applications also have to deal with and which will probably be solved in the foreseeable future.

Alternative possibilities: As with many blockchain alternatives, a not purely decentralized system could also be used here. Instead, a unified distributed system would be conceivable. Furthermore, the legal system would have to recognize the information on the blockchain as legally binding, as is the case with the other applications.

Practical examples: Currently, I do not know of any examples where a blockchain is used for this application but people often integrate hashes from timestamps as a message into other blockchains in order to have additional proof of their patent, even if this proof would probably not yet be legally binding today. Whether I would trust a company today to successfully establish patent protection via a blockchain, I do not dare to say completely. I almost believe that such an innovation must come from governments themselves in order to set a standard. Many of the applications in this chapter benefit not only from the clear ownership of a blockchain, but also from other advantages of a distributed system. The next chapter deals with privacy and its applications.

BLOCKCHAIN APPLICATION 2: DATA PROTECTION

Through anonymization and partial intransparency a blockchain offers an impenetrable privacy for everyone and everything.

We have already discussed the issue of privacy in a blockchain elsewhere in this book. The point here is to combine anonymity, i.e. the knowledge of who is behind an address, with transparency, i.e. the knowledge of which processes are stored on a blockchain. In the section on cryptocurrencies, you have learned about the counterarguments, such as money laundering. This chapter now deals with blockchain applications for problems which have not yet been solved due to a lack of privacy, or which could be significantly improved and made more secure by the blockchain.

MEDICINE (PATIENT DATA, PRESCRIPTIONS, VACCINATION CERTIFICATES …)

Problem description: This blockchain application is particularly close to my heart because it brought me into the blockchain world as an ex-doctor in 2014. All too often I have experienced unconscious patients coming into trauma surgery and we knew nothing about their patient history. No information about allergies, previous illnesses, nothing! Hopefully you have never had to go to hospital because of a serious accident. But perhaps you have already asked yourself why you have to undergo the same examinations over and over again and why your doctor cannot simply save a laboratory report or an X-ray and make it available to other doctors. It is the decades-long struggle between data protection versus the provision of information. Actually, it would be a huge advantage if all tests, images and findings were stored about us. If we then went to a doctor, he could retrieve all information with our permission at the push of a button. So he wouldn't need to get the information from repeated medical tests that many other doctors before him have probably already got. But the statement „with our permission" poses a certain problem. Our own medical data is enormously valuable. If this information falls into the wrong hands, a person, for example, could suddenly be uninsurable. Because an insurance company could conclude that due to his entire medical history, combined with his genetic disposition, he has a much too high risk of illness X or Y. If credit card details are stolen from a server, this is annoying, but you can simply block your card and apply for a new one. But if your genetic information or your medical history falls into unauthorized hands, you cannot simply change or invalidate it. You then have to live with the fact that companies use them against you. The challenges in the field of medical data storage are a prime example of how to weigh up the enormous benefits against a worst-case scenario: In fact, every patient would have a data registry of this kind for himself in order to give a treating physician the maximum amount of information he needs for a reliable diagnosis, therapy or complaint relief. However, the potential risk of data misuse is far too high. So far, there is no convincing solution, and in times of the General Data Protection Regulation (GDPR) this endeavor seems to be to move even further away. If it weren't for the blockchain technology…

Solution explanation: The decentralized data storage possibilities of a blockchain are made for this problem. If, for example, one million users have data worth 1 billion USD on a company's centralized server, it would be enough for an attacker to invest 900 million USD to make a profit of 100 million USD. This makes it incredibly difficult to secure centralized servers. The more people use a service, the riskier it becomes for everyone. In a decentralized system, the exact opposite is the case due to the privacy offered. With a blockchain there is no server that can be hacked. Data is stored decentrally by everyone. In order to get there, every single private-key-public-key pair of users has to be hacked. Let's assume that one million users also store data worth 1,000 USD per user. This data with a total value of 1 billion USD is not stored in a single place however. It is distributed among the users. The maximum that an attacker can get out of this is 1,000 USD per attack. At the same time, in the case of blockchain an attack costs almost as much as an attack on a large server. Even if such an attack would cost only one thousandth, this 100,000 USD attack would bring a loss of 99,000 USD. So it would never be worthwhile to try a hack on such a decentralized system. The privacy of a blockchain therefore represents an optimal solution for medicine. A patient creates a private key, stores his data completely anonymously, and if he is with a doctor, only the patient himself can decrypt the data. These are the advantages of a system that can be accessed from anywhere and at the same time offers the certainty that nobody can access the data except the rightful owner of the private key. However, there are still a few challenges that need to be mastered.

Challenges: The challenges are not different from those already discussed for other applications. On the one hand, the question of data storage capacity has to be solved. Laboratory reports, scans and documents require enormous storage space, which is not yet available on the blockchain. In addition, the generation of private keys is a challenge, as is the case with decentralized identity verification. How to generate? How to save? How to secure? How to retrieve? The differences define, for example, whether the private key of a patient can also be retrieved if the patient is unconscious, or whether it can only be used if the patient consciously decides to authorize it. Finally, the question of a standard is justified. Because only if one agrees on this somehow, one's own data can be read by all potentially involved physicians.

Alternative possibilities: For the first time I don't see a centralized application as an alternative for a possible blockchain application. For cryptocurrencies as well as for many other applications, this is always a point of discussion. With our data I rather see the opposite. I dare to claim that the risk of centralized competition is practically eliminated here. The only alternative that I see is that you don't use a blockchain, but that every patient somehow stores his own data himself or keeps it with him. If we humans merge more and more with machines in the future, something like this is also conceivable in digital form. One could implant a contactless chip on which all data is stored and can be retrieved again. So nothing would be stored in the cloud, and only the patient himself would have access to the data. If that sounds too futuristic to you, then let me tell you: I have already met people personally who are already doing this for health prevention. Much of what sounds crazy today can be quite normal in 20 years. Just think of social media etc. As an entrepreneur it is important to see such waves coming. The disadvantage of such a chip implantation solution would be the lack of redundancy: If the chip is broken or lost, the data is gone forever. This would be impossible with a blockchain. So there might be a combination of the two at the very beginning? We'll see.

Practical examples: There are already many approaches being tried out. Almost every day I receive requests from startups whether I would like to work as an advisor (consultant). Even if I had great interest, I could only participate if such a startup had already been formed a little and had a clear idea for its implementation. Personally, I would start here with a niche for patients and start, for example, with vaccination passport data or prescriptions. Anyone who has ever lost their vaccination passport knows how annoying this is. To store the vaccination data would not be too difficult of a blockchain application. It would be a good proof of concept, which could be extended to other areas later. If you already have some good implementations here, please feel free to contact me and my team. Details can be found in the entrepreneur's chapter at the end. In any case, healthcare companies and chip manufacturers should take a close look at these things. The first sections on blockchain applications are usually a bit longer. The following sections, on the other hand, are based on similar principles in other areas, and the description of the advantages and disadvantages can partly be omitted. This means that the next sections can be shorter. Let's take a look at the topic of data protection in communication, social media and passwords in the next section.

COMMUNICATION (WHATSAPP, E-MAIL, SMS ...)

Problem description: Similar to other data protection applications, trust is an essential problem in electronic communication. Too often one hears how the US secret service NSA reads e-mails, taps messages and records telephone calls. In addition, centralized authorities can prevent communication, which has already occurred more frequently during riots.

Solution explanation: A blockchain could decentralize communication and thus deprive a company of the power to either read out communication data itself, forward it to government authorities or block it. The process is the same as with other blockchain applications. Instead of running everything on a centralized server, information is routed decentrally so that nobody has the data themselves. This means that no one can block, read or pass on the data. The most important challenge here is the same as with decentralized peer-to-peer systems (computer networks without centralized computers) for routing: The number of possible routing options increases exponentially with each additional subscriber. If there are four users, A, B, C, D, there are six routing options (3+2+1). With five participants, there are already ten possibilities and with six participants 15. An optimal communication channel is no longer possible from a relatively manageable number of participants without a central routing point, which controls the transfer of information. Therefore both the transmission speed and the scaling possibilities suffer in such a system.

Alternative possibilities: While such a system would be conceivable for basic text transmission, it is more likely to be a centralized communication solution with excellent end-to-end communication. Similar solutions have been developed in the case of Signal, WhatsApp and Pretty Good Privacy (PGP). If the corresponding solution runs on an open source system, as Signal does, for example, it cannot simply be blocked by a state.

Practical examples: From my point of view, most blockchain companies in the „communications sector" are currently on the wrong track rather than on the way to solving a real problem. Nevertheless, e-mail providers and message programs should look at such decentralized solutions. Maybe a part of the communication which is not so data intensive can be offered decentralized in order to profit from the advantages of a blockchain.

SOCIAL MEDIA AND SEARCH ENGINES (FACEBOOK, GOOGLE ...)

Problem description: For obvious reasons, social media and search engines often become the focus of data protection. For users, the use of Facebook, Google and Co. is supposedly free of charge. But as we just witnessed in 2017 the mess that Facebook caused with the data theft, we all pay with our privacy. Apart from that, the question often arises as to how social media platforms could arm themselves against being abused by individual users or user groups, for example to influence elections and the like.

Solution explanation: Blockchain is the perfect solution. On the one hand, a user does not hand over his own data, on the other hand there is no centralized unit that could censor photos, posts or videos. Whoever provides the content could also be directly involved in the advertising revenue. This could lead to a win-win situation in which operators, creators and users could win in equal measure.

Challenges: What sounds good in theory is often difficult to put into practice. People simply act very irresponsibly when they realize that they can do anything with impunity. Thus, many racist and anti-religious contents are uploaded to the current decentralized social media platforms, which would immediately be censored on centralized platforms. Since the uploaders cannot be located, the question arises how this should be prevented in the future. The bad content also shows an inertia effect: people like to use networks whereas many of their friends and acquaintances as possible are as well. Other platforms are only used if there is enough drive to change. As a content creator, you also only offer your content where you meet most consumers and where you have the greatest financial or economic impact.

Alternative possibilities: Google, Facebook and Co. will definitely offer their centralized solutions for even longer. As long as there is a suitable balance between privacy and performance, this will not change for a long time to come. Personally, I am therefore very skeptical about decentralized social media platforms. Offering them sounds good in theory, but in practice they bring with them many problems which centralized platforms do not have.

Practical examples: There are already several decentralized proof of concepts. But regardless of whether they are decentralized blogs, video platforms, Instagram competitors or podcast sites, they are all currently failing due to a lack of interest and quality. I believe that this will improve at some point. But this will take much longer than some predict. Because the inertia of a network counteracts any innovation here. Let's see if the existing social media companies and search engines can afford such a drastic blunder at some point that people are willing to switch to other decentralized platforms and accept their problems.

DATA AND PASSWORDS
(CREDIT CARD DATA, ACCESS DATA...)

Problem description: In addition to the applications already mentioned, there are of course many others that could benefit from perfect data protection. The question of how to store one's password or other accesses in a highly secure manner has existed for a long time; and all existing passwords and access data represent an attractive target for centralized systems.

Solution: Decentralized systems could, for example, secure all passwords with their own private key. Since this happens simultaneously on all computers, a hacker attack would be practically impossible.

Challenges: Solving this problem via blockchain requires a great deal of clarification, so that more and more people are becoming aware of the problems with passwords, credit card data, etc. Especially with purely digital applications, many of the physical challenges, such as identity, are eliminated. For this reason, blockchains would be particularly suitable.

Alternative possibilities: But if, for example, you lose the private key to your decentralized password manager, then that's it with the passwords. Here it may be necessary to use one or the other combined solution in order not to cause a knockout to the user.

Practical examples: Data protection is becoming more and more important; and the more hacks and negative messages there are in centralized services, the more likely I am to give startups in this area a chance. If you start in a strategic niche in the digital domain, the physical challenges of other blockchain applications are non-existent, and the advantages of a blockchain come to light. In addition to password managers, readers should think of all the services they use themselves and have to enter their data into. How could they be decentralized? The best ideas often emerge from solving one's own problem. After the huge area of application „data protection" we now come to the next big application group: the smart contracts.

BLOCKCHAIN APPLICATION 3: SMART CONTRACTS

If digital contracts are combined with a blockchain, an entire community ensures that these so-called smart contracts are guaranteed to be executed.

Nick Szabo was the first to introduce the term smart contract in 1994, describing a process in which a contract is implemented by a digital program with the support of a community. The blockchain thus assumes the function of a new third party. Where such smart contracts can be applied, I describe in this chapter.

TRUSTEESHIP (NOTARIES, LAWYERS, EBAY)

Problem description: The problem of trusteeship is obvious to everyone. The same concept has prevailed for every transfer of value in which the other party is not trusted: The two persons involved in the contract use a neutral third party who first receives the money from the buyer for a purchase, for example, and then confirms receipt of the money to the seller. Then the seller can confidently hand over the goods to the buyer, because as soon as the buyer confirms receipt of the goods, the neutral third party will give the money to the seller. Regardless of whether it is a real estate purchase, eBay auctions or numerous other applications: The procedure is always similar, but the problems resulting from it are also always similar: Such a third party must be really trustworthy and neutral. It also costs money, and it is not always easy to find such a party.

Solution explanation: A blockchain can help here in the simplest way: a contract is defined as a smart contract in which two parties consider one or more causes and one or more consequences. If A happens, the smart contract makes sure that B follows („If you give me this, you get it guaranteed!"). This is also possible with more than two contracting parties („Give person 1, 2 and 3 XXX to person 4, so it is ensured that person 5 YYY to person 6, 7 and 8."). Smart contracts can therefore easily be made quite complex and replace a neutral third party. The details are recorded with the help of the blockchain and supported by an entire community.

Challenges: The main challenge of such smart contracts is to use them for non-digital contractual objects. Currently, they only work for digital things. „If you send me file X, then you get sum Y", works well as a smart contract, because everything can be tracked digitally and can therefore be programmed easily as an if-then-loop. It becomes more difficult when it comes to physical things that do not (yet) have access to the blockchain without a third party. For example, if it's about the physical book X and the paper money sum Y, it might not be possible to verify without a referee whether you gave me the book and I really gave you the agreed paper notes for it. Furthermore, the value within the smart contract can develop completely independent of the value of the blockchain. This can lead to problems in the warranty process. Let's say we make a bet on the number of sunny days in a year. For every sunny day you get 1,000 USD from me, for every rainy day I get 1,000 USD from you. If the statistics suggest a 50/50 distribution, it is unlikely that ever a large imbalance forms. So we don't need a large, strong community like a blockchain guarantees. Because even though it may sometimes be a matter of a few thousand USD, on average the sums paid to each other should always balance each other out to zero over time. Sometimes you owe me, sometimes I owe you. What if there are 100 sunny days in a row? The smart contract would then be worth 100,000 USD. If, however, the community had only set a value of 50,000 USD by consensus, the loser of the smart contract could make a profit out of bribing the blockchain participants and making the smart contract null and void. Blockchains normally have an inherent value, and this usually leads to a joint increase or decrease in value. With smart contracts, however, this can develop completely independently of the rest and create problems.

Alternative possibilities: There are alternatives to smart contracts only insofar as trustworthy centralized third parties are involved.

Practical examples: As already mentioned frequently, there are enough areas of application. Fiduciary agencies should definitely take a look at this technology. Online mail order companies such as Amazon, eBay, Alibaba, etc., should also definitely look into smart contracts. One reason why so many people like to use PayPal is the possible reimbursement of money paid in a rip-off. Smart contracts would be a great application here, especially as such a system could be combined with postal delivery. In this way, the dispatch and receipt of a delivery could be documented in a relatively new way. The real estate market, which is worth billions, will also be revolutionized by smart contracts if you no longer need a trustee for a million dollar deal. In the future, however, issues such as ransom demands could also be addressed.

DECENTRALIZED COMPUTER PROGRAMS (REGULATED PLATFORMS...)

Problem description: Apart from being used as a trustee substitute, smart contracts can be used as decentralized computer programs. Today, every computer program runs either on a centralized computer or on a server. If this fails or is switched off, the program no longer runs. Cloud servers, which are distributed, can partially solve the failure problem. But what if, for example, a government no longer allows a certain program and wants to switch it off?

Solution explanation: This is precisely where decentralized computer programs can help and run as smart contracts on thousands of computers at the same time. The currently largest decentralized computer Ethereum offers its users exactly this and has already established standards which hobby programmers can use. By implementing „Turing Complete" at Ethereum, even quite complex applications could be designed, which can then no longer be stopped by anyone.

Challenges: The biggest challenge here is resource capacity. More complex computer programs require an enormous amount of computing power, which must be available and usable on all computers simultaneously. This is the main reason why only basic applications have been used so far.

Alternative possibilities: Some alternatives to a completely decentralized blockchain go the way of an incomplete decentralization. This allows a much better scaling than Ethereum, for example. However, the question is rightly raised as to the extent to which these solutions are resistant to censorship and whether they are better than a fully centralized implementation.

Practical examples: There are many possible applications. No matter whether ERC20 or ERC721 contracts on Ethereum, whether decentralized stock exchanges or alternatives to the prohibited Megaupload: Companies all over the world are looking at fields of application in the decentralized computing sector. However, it will be essential whether such applications are used for legal or illegal purposes. If decentralized stock exchanges are used exclusively to conclude illegal contracts, the governments will somehow try to intervene, as they have done with Megaupload. Just as dynamite can be used for road building, but also for warfare, decentralization is about using it for the right purpose and not abusing it for criminal or dangerous machinations.

BETTING (BETTING OFFICES, LOTTERY OFFICES…)

Problem description: Betting is an interesting use of smart contracts. If you look at the basic constellation of a bet, you can see that two or more parties agree on different results for certain events. But what if one party does not stick to the agreement?

Solution explanation: Smart contracts find a simple implementation here. Instead of securing a bet by a third party, its compliance can be ensured decentrally by a blockchain. Depending on the size of the bet, this can even be significantly cheaper and more reliable. Profit probabilities could arise automatically from supply and demand via the open market. In some cases, for example, much better odds would be possible than those set by a centralized party for betting agencies.

Challenges: In addition to the challenges described above for all smart contracts, the question arises as to what is being bet on with the help of decentralized blockchain technology. If nobody bears the responsibility, who will make sure that nothing immoral is betted on? What if a bet is placed on the death of a person?

Alternative possibilities: Questions about ethics have not yet been clarified unambiguously, and perhaps they can never be clarified. Thus bets can perhaps only be settled decentrally in theory, but they will practically never be implemented.

Practical examples: However, there are a few examples of applications. It doesn't matter whether you place censorship-free bets on presidential candidates or bet on yourself: the relevance would be enormous, as long as it is about legal and morally unobjectionable things. For example, you could bet that you could create Project X. Other people can bet against you because they think you can't do it. Depending on the probability and the amount of profit, a fair distribution of penalties and rewards could be created for all those involved. If, for example, you bet 1,000 USD that you create something quite improbable, and 1,000 people bet 10 USD each against it, then an interesting incentive arises to give your best and also to create it. If you really make it, you get the 10,000 USD. If you don't make it, you lose 1,000 USD. Next, let us talk about a special form of betting, namely casinos.

GAMBLING (CASINOS, POKER ...)

Problem description: In casinos nothing else happens than betting on certain probabilities. Internet casinos are becoming more and more popular, especially in the online sector, as this way the state monopoly on gambling, which exists in most countries, can be circumvented. But how can a user ensure that an online casino does not manipulate the odds? How do you know that everything is really fair? For example, in the case of a computer victory in a card game, how do you know whether the computer involved knew the cards of its real opponent and therefore won? What if an online casino is simply locked and the money bet is gone? In the online sector, users place 100 percent of their trust in the centralized party.

Solution explanation: A blockchain with smart contracts could easily solve this: Rules and probabilities are disclosed completely transparently via the blockchain, and everyone can see from the smart contracts that these are also implemented in the existing form. So there is guaranteed no more fraud in the form that casinos say one thing, but then do something completely different. In an online card game, the cards could be split transparently by a shuffling machine with open source code. Each player sees that the other player has correctly dealt cards. However, nobody can access the cards of the other player, because they are masked by their own secret key. At the end, the keys can be revealed; and each participant can clearly see that at the money was not stolen and that everything was done fairly. In addition, the blockchain would always give you the money you had invested yourself. An online casino couldn't simply get away with taking advantage of players.

Challenges: Once everything in an online casino or online betting office is running on the Internet, this application is actually predestined for blockchain technology. All those casinos that already offer this online are on the move in one of the few businesses that have an active business model. The biggest challenge here is to comply with the regulations of the legislator. So you should be prepared for legal disputes if you want to found a company in this area.

Alternative possibilities: I see here quite few alternatives to a blockchain. As there will be gambling for a long time to come, this is certainly also an attractive, but not innovative area of decentralization.

Practical examples: We have already discussed the various application examples in the solutions. The question for you is whether you simply want to earn a little money by offering such an online casino, or whether you really want to generate added value for the companies. These online bets are flowing into a different area of application - that of insurance. But in order to do that, we first have to talk about forecasts.

ORACLE
(EXPERT OPINION, EXPERT ADVICE, ...)

Problem description: So far we have mainly concentrated on use cases, where blockchains create trust decentrally within a community. But how do these blockchains communicate with their environment? For example, if we look at a bet on the weather and say: „If the sun shines tomorrow at 12:00 noon, you pay me 100 USD; if it's cloudy, I pay you 100 USD". We can enter this smart contract on a blockchain, but how does the blockchain community decide decentrally whether the sun was shining or not? The blockchain itself does not know, unless there is another trustworthy decentralized possibility, for example in the form of 500 sensors connected to the blockchain. These would then clearly determine whether the sun is shining or not. Until such a technology works, however, the legitimate question arises as to how information is introduced into the blockchain from an area outside the blockchain without trust. It is therefore a question of how a community in which nobody bears the responsibility can integrate new information from outside into the community without having to trust a single party. We have already mentioned this problem in many blockchain applications, and here I would like to discuss a few of the possible solutions.

Solution explanation: The currently most practiced solution is that of a so-called oracle, even if it is not yet really in use. An oracle is based on a game theoretical trick: one disconnects an electoral system from the outcome of the decision. Several participants vote retrospectively on the outcome of the event on which a bet was placed in advance. There is a reward for those who lie with the majority of the decision. So if we use the example of the sun bet, of the two times 100 USD bet, for example, 5 percent, i.e. 10 USD, is spent on the oracle. An algorithm randomly selects a group from the blockchain participants that is as small as possible but as large as necessary. For example, in this case there could be ten persons. They represent the oracle, and their task is to find out the truth - in the example, to find out whether the sun shone or not. The time at which the oracle becomes active must be as close as possible to the time to which the bet refers. At the same time, however, the oracle must have enough time for the measurement or the casting of his vote.

In our case, for example, this would be one hour before. Each of the randomly selected people then looks up whether the sun is shining or not, and each of them gives his opinion. What the majority decides is then determined as a fact, which the blockchain accepts as new information.

In order for the oracle to vote „correctly" as best it can, the 10 USD reward is divided among all oracle members who belong to the majority. Suppose, of the ten people one person does not vote at all, and of the other nine five say that the sun had shone, and four that it was cloudy. So the five people correspond to the majority and divide the 10 USD so that everyone gets 2 USD. Of course, the oracle members must not know each other. In addition, the election time must be as short as possible, so that oracles try to find out the „truth" in their own interest as a whole. Everyone wants to be with the majority, which hopefully finds out the truth in order to get the reward. Of course there is justified criticism of this model.

Challenges: On the one hand, the question arises with oracles as to whether people really try to vote correctly, or whether they simply try to trick the system by voting independently of the truth according to what the others presumably recognize as the truth. However, if there is enough anonymization here, nobody should be able to guess which vote others are voting for. Each participant must then really be able to vote for „the truth" vote. If there is additionally a multiplicity of simultaneous votes, for example 1,000 oracle tasks in each hour, and remains thereby unknown, which purpose the respective oracle serves, then hopefully each oracle member should focus on finding out the „truth". Only then the chance exists to belong to the majority and to get the reward. In terms of game theory, oracles would be conceptually possible especially with high oracle numbers.

Nevertheless, the question also arises whether the majority is always right - or whether a small group of experts is coming far closer to the truth. If you look at stock markets and compare the decisions of investment guru Warren Buffett with those of the masses, you are definitely better advised to invest your money like Buffett and not like the masses of investors. It is difficult to assess whether this is the case with all questions or whether this only applies to expert questions. However, an expert concept may also emerge for oracles, in which certain people are better suited than others to specific questions according to their reputation.

The final challenge is that of decentralization. This is actually desirable. But an oracle, like other decentralized systems, will always be slower and more expensive than a centralized system. Thus, in my opinion, an oracle will not prevail for small trivial things, but rather for larger, essential questions on which it is not possible to agree on an independent arbitrator. However, there are several alternatives to oracles.

Alternative possibilities: The first alternative remains a centralized confirmation process. As long as there is enough trust, there is no further way. Another possibility would be the confirmation of the facts by a whole cascade of small confirmations. If we talk about transparency blockchains in the next chapters, this concept will occur even more frequently in logistics or other application areas. The idea is simple: it does not require a centralized party to confirm an entire event, but rather a series of many different parties, each confirming a small part of the larger one. For example, in order to confirm a domestic fire, which we will discuss in the insurance example in the next section, we will therefore not rely on the final statement of an individual insurance expert, but rather on a confirmation from the fire brigade, from the responsible municipality, from an independent expert, etc. They all confirm that the fire has been confirmed. They all confirm part of the overall event: that there was a fire, when the fire brigade left, what damage was caused, etc. This could be used to create a logic in which, for example, at least six out of ten possible parties would have to agree, since the facts of the case would actually be confirmed on the blockchain. Admittedly, there is still a slight centralized dependence. However, there is more transparency and a greater distribution than with a purely centralized alternative.

Practical examples: It remains to be seen to what extent oracles or transparent confirmation chains will prevail as alternatives. The fact that something works in theory does not mean that this is the case in practice. The sun bet is probably a bad example because the procedure for such an application is too slow, too expensive and probably also too irrelevant. However, it is precisely this example that is often cited by companies doing research in this field. A wonderful sounding solution for a completely irrelevant problem can be found more frequently in the blockchain area. However, the future will definitely bring a direct blockchain interoperability in which oracles are no longer needed. Blockchains can then communicate directly with each other. Nevertheless, I would never completely write off oracles as a solution. Especially for larger consensus problems, they can be used as an optimal decentralized solution.

INSURANCES (CLAIMS, SETTLEMENTS...)

Problem description: An insurance policy is nothing more than a bet on an event. The exciting thing about an insurance bet, however, is that both betting parties are actually hoping for the same outcome. This may sound surprising, but think of a house that is worth 250,000 USD, for example. The house owner does not take out insurance because he speculates that this house will burn down. Rather, he hopes that it will not burn down. In the unlikely event, however, that it should burn down anyway, he wants to be insured and in the event of damage receive the sum insured of 250,000 USD. Who is the counterparty to the bet? The insurer. This company does not believe either that said house burns down. So why does such a bet work when both parties actually hope for the same outcome?

First, it works because an insurance company calculates the probabilities for the fire better than the policyholder. Second, such a bet is based on the fact that it is made not only with one person, but also with many others. The bet that an insurance company makes is therefore based on the assumption that although a house will burn down at some point, it will not necessarily be a specific house. Through this calculation in combination with probabilities, a mostly highly lucrative business model is created. Because with an intersection that is large enough, the existing risks balance each other out. In this way, each individual can insure himself, and the insurance also benefits.

What challenges can a blockchain solve for insurance companies? As with any company, the customer pays the company costs and the insurer's profits in form of a monthly or annual premium. In order to insure a house for 250,000 USD, for example, he pays 100 USD per month as an insurance fee. However, the insurer keeps 50 USD as profit for himself. Only the other 50 USD go into the pool of reserves, with which the insured houses are protected against fire or other damage. If there were an alternative to the result of this special bet, then a policyholder could save half of the costs and would still have the same insurance advantage. Furthermore, the centralization of an insurance company, as with all centralized institutions, can lead to arbitrary decisions, which can be negative for the customer. Many of us have already heard of cases in which an insurance company, following a report of damage, extricates itself from its responsibilities and invokes clauses in order to not have to pay. This is the nightmare of every insured person. Wouldn't it be great to include a completely neutral party that firstly costs very little and secondly guarantees settlement by the insurance company in the event of a claim?

Solution explanation: The solution is a smart contract on the blockchain. Just as an insurance algorithm calculates the costs for an insurance policy, so can someone program this for a smart contract. No company is necessary for this; theoretically a smart teenager can do it in his own bedroom. Accordingly, the costs would not amount to 50 percent, but only to 1 percent of the premium paid. In addition, the algorithms and costs can be displayed completely transparently on the blockchain. Anyone who uses the smart contract as an insurance policy knows what they are getting into. In addition, the smart contract will hopefully not only be used by one person, but by thousands or millions of people. In this way, a well-distributed pool of reserves is created, which can easily cover the payments from the circle of depositors. In order to insure the house of 250,000 USD, one does not need to pay 100 USD, but perhaps only 60 USD per month. This not only means enormous cost savings, but also the guarantee that the insurance company will also pay if damage occurs, as the smart contract is guaranteed to be implemented.

Challenges: the justified question is, of course, how does the smart contract know that damage has actually occurred? Here we come again to the problem of communication between a blockchain and the physical environment, which we have already addressed several times. Until blockchains can communicate with each other, the already mentioned oracles or divisions of responsibility will be indispensable. This is by no means a perfect solution and it ultimately also depends on it whether decent solutions can prevail in insurance companies or not. A further problem with every decentralized solution is by definition the question of who is responsible. With insurance, however, this can have drastic consequences. Here is an example:

If I pay my 60 USD per month into the smart contract to insure my house with a damage sum of 250,000 USD, the smart contract cannot judge whether I insure my house or another. Now you might ask why I should insure another house. Well, neighbor A sees what I'm doing and says: „Very nice, I'll pay 60 USD now and insure your house. If your house burns down, I also get 250,000 USD." Neighbor B does that too. Neighbor C, D, E, etc. as well. Suddenly the original insurance becomes a bet, where many people get 250.000 USD each time, when my house burns down. An event, which should be unlikely, could become now probable, since numerous people would have an advantage of it, if my house would burn down. Imagine what it would be like with life insurance if you had a 1-million-USD policy and suddenly other people started betting on people's deaths. This would completely revive the contract killing business.

With centralized systems, someone has the responsibility, and therefore the power to prohibit such scenarios. Decentralized systems lack such a control option. This often leads to scenarios that were not originally considered. However, such scenarios are often not thought through by companies that want to offer decentralized insurance solutions. Therefore the question is quite justified whether the conceivable alternatives prevail.

Alternative possibilities: When it comes to cost optimization in insurance, many online insurers now offer a slim mobile or web variant without a large overhead due to staff overhangs or huge marketing budgets. Such solutions, albeit centralized, definitely represent an attractive alternative to decentralized solutions, as long as the centralized insurers do not abuse the trust of their customers. A benevolent and just dictator would still be the most effective system.

Practical examples: Theoretically, of course, any kind of insurance could be revolutionized by such a decentralized system, regardless of whether it is life or property insurance. However, as soon as blockchain-based companies improve oracles and incorporate certain rules into smart contracts, this would be a clear challenge to centralized insurance companies. Since some companies are already working on these things, I can only recommend that every classic insurer set up a department to deal with blockchain and decentralization issues. Just as horse-drawn carriages have been replaced by cars, a decentralized system could send centralized insurance companies to the eternal hunting grounds. While this scenario could happen, it does not necessarily have to happen, and this fact should not be underestimated. All too often one hears false statements about the fact that the insurance industry is guaranteed to be revolutionized by blockchains. There is no guarantee. Or like my mom would say: 'Guarantees only exist when buying a toaster.' So each of these statements in the blockchain area should be rationally checked for plausibility.

CROWDFUNDING AND ICOS (FUNDING PLATFORMS, PRIVATE EQUITY INVESTMENTS ...)

Problem description: Companies always need capital. If a company is still young, this is particularly important, but it is precisely then that it is difficult to find. Especially since there are questions about transparency, trust and clear rules, investors want to understand, what the invested money is used for.

Solution explanation: Decentralized fundraising via a blockchain can help here. The blockchain makes it transparent for every investor to see what happens to the money invested. The company concerned can issue its own token, which either serves a purpose as a utility token in the project or promises financial advantages as a security token. These so-called Initial Coin Offerings (ICOs) or Token Sales have enjoyed great popularity since 2014. The company's own tokens are linked as a smart contract to the exchange of another cryptocurrency, and so a company receives bitcoin in return for its own token, for example.

I'm one of their biggest fans of this application, but also a critic because I've used it myself, and I see it repeatedly abused by entrepreneurs.

Challenges: There are still some challenges around ICOs. This raises the question of regulation. Is there a need for legislation or rules to protect customers, or are none necessary? Currently there are too many people in a gold-rush mood who use ICOs for scammy projects, which then collapse. The investors are then left with nothing. I personally do not like complete deregulation however, a view I clearly express to working groups of the European Union. I believe the regulator should rather state what is allowed and what is not. At the end of this book there is a whole chapter on how you as an entrepreneur can use ICOs for yourself. In my book "Cryptocurrencies simply explained" there are also some detailed pros and cons of ICOs. You can find it here: http://cryptofit.community

Alternative possibilities: Investment rounds can continue to be organized centrally. Whether ICOs or decentralized funding will prevail remains to be seen.

Practical examples: There are always enough theoretical fields for crowdfunding: On the one hand as funding for startups within the framework of ICOs, and on the other hand to replace IPOs (Initial Public Offering for stock corporations) in an advanced stage. For example, in order to carry out an IPO, you need millions as a company. For an ICO, most of the times only a few thousand USD are needed. So an ICO would be an attractive alternative even for larger companies. Peer-to-peer lending platforms should also look at decentralized opportunities, as the costs here could be significantly lower than with the current centralized opportunities. Whether and how this will influence investment funds in the future remains to be seen. Because: even if ICOs could assert themselves, this does not mean that venture capital funds will disappear. It simply means that they will have to adapt.

GLOBAL AGREEMENTS (INTERGOVERNMENTAL CONTRACTS, INTERNATIONAL COURT OF JUSTICE)

Problem description: Global agreements could be represented excellently by a blockchain. Global institutions such as the International Court of Justice or intergovernmental treaties are always secured in one place. Ultimately, therefore, they are always subject to a different interest, even if this is not intended. It is always difficult to take action against the hand that feeds you.

Solution explanation: These global contracts could be secured via smart contracts on the blockchain, whereby the blockchain itself could be supported jointly by all countries. It would then be incredibly expensive for the participants not to keep to contracts or regulations that have been agreed upon once they have been concluded.

Challenges: However, the large countries, which usually control the world's centralized institutions, would first have to accept a decentralized solution. Whether and how this should work remains to be seen.

Alternative possibilities: There are no real alternatives, but it is always difficult to get states and organizations to give up power.

Practical examples: Just when Argentina, for example, no longer wanted to repay its own debts, a smart contract would have been helpful. A pure bankruptcy would not have been so easy, because the smart contract would have forced the implementation of the contract, i.e. the repayment of debts, as best as possible. However, I do not believe that a private company can implement such a mammoth project, but rather that the initiative must come from the states themselves. When, if and how is, of course, more than questionable.

COURTS
(JURISPRUDENCE, COURTS OF ARBITRATION)

Problem description: The next area leads us in a completely different direction: the legal system. Often one hears about missing decisions of judges, intransparent rules that are incomprehensible, about bribery and bias. Wouldn't it be great if instead of a single person a complete fair and smart process would decide on right and wrong?

Solution explanation: The concept of smart contracts could be introduced into the legal system. Instead of letting judges judge on a case, the law could be programmed as computer code. The cases could be processed extremely quickly, cheaply and efficiently.

Challenges: Whether this is more a theoretical application case or one that can really be put into practice depends on some difficult questions, above all whether smart contracts can ever be built so complex that we feel comfortable for a computer to decide about people. How would the collection of evidence work here? How would the evaluation of circumstantial evidence work? These are just two of the questions that arise in this context.

Alternative possibilities: Even if the application case is dreamt of by some visionary judge, I am very skeptical about it. The legal system is very agile, and once programmed smart contracts are difficult to change. Therefore, I believe that judges and lawyers will not have to fear competition from blockchain for a long time to come. It is more likely that the trend will be towards online advice, resulting in a better cost structure and efficiency.

Practical examples: However, if the application of artificial intelligence becomes reality, a judge on the blockchain with all the advantages and disadvantages of such a solution is a possibility for the near future.

ARTIFICIAL INTELLIGENCE
(CLOUDS, COMPUTERS ...)

Problem description: If we think smart contracts further, we inevitably come to the concept that a smart contract system that is complex enough can lead to artificial intelligence (AI). One question that arises again and again with the thought concept of artificial intelligence is: Can human intelligence generate an AI at all? Centralized systems for this are often seen as a limitation, which would not give an AI enough possibilities for development.

Solution explanation: Since a blockchain system is decentralized, the AI here would also have every possibility of expansion, without being able to be restricted by a centralized power.

Challenges: The challenge of a decentralized AI is obvious and concerns AI in general: without going into a moral discussion about pros and cons of AIs, one can say in summary that there are still many open questions about the feasibility of a generalized AI. This is independent of the question of whether it is used centralized or decentralized.

Alternative possibilities: Especially in such cases, in which the implementation of a centralized execution does not really help, the word „blockchain" is apparently used more frequently to help with marketing and financing.

Whether and how an alternative solution is possible here thanks to blockchain is difficult to say so far.

Practical examples: Too often I see at blockchain events how a startup announces its next breakthrough in the field of AI. It quickly becomes apparent that the startups in question have already failed in centralized implementation and are now simply doing fundraising by using the term blockchain.

Centralized companies like Google have been doing research in this area for quite some time. That's why I don't think a blockchain is really needed here. For this reason I wouldn't rely on a startup here, but rather on companies like Google or Facebook. Whether an AI system developed by them will later run on a blockchain is something I can imagine. But this has nothing to do with the false promises of some companies in this area. However, AI solutions bring us to an application that should perhaps be seen as a potential warning in the blockchain field.

SKYNET (TERMINATOR ...)

Problem description: Whether Skynet[19] solves a problem or not can be discussed at length. Nevertheless, it is (still) a theoretical AI application, which is the main antagonist in the Terminator movies. The solution to the problem it should solve is to eliminate mankind. Sounds great, doesn't it?

Solution explanation: Herewith a clear warning is to be expressed regarding a decentralized AI. Many visionary thinkers, including myself, see a potential Skynet as an absolute possibility resulting from AI on a blockchain. I will repeat this later in the chapter on threats. Such an AI could copy itself completely decentrally into every server, every robot and every machine and thus control them decentrally. Should such an AI really no longer be disconnectable and gain self-awareness, it can, as fictionally depicted in the Terminator movies, try to eliminate mankind - and will probably do so successfully.

Challenges: The real challenges here do not lie in the blockchain area, but rather in the application of artificial intelligence.

Alternative possibilities: Personally, I hope that there will be alternatives to a Skynet and that a malicious AI will never get onto a blockchain.

Practical examples: That doesn't mean that I'm against artificial intelligence, but rather that companies like Google

---
19 https://en.wikipedia.org/wiki/Skynet_(Terminator)

have to be clearly aware of the possibilities, but also the dangers, of AI. Fortunately, we are still a bit away from creating a generalized AI at all. That's why I don't worry too much here yet and enjoy every day when no robot has made me its slave.

BLOCKCHAIN APPLICATION 4: TOKENIZATION

If any value is represented as a token on a blockchain, an unprecedented compatibility between different asset classes is created.

SECURITIES (EQUITIES, BONDS…)

Problem description: If one wants to sell or exchange securities such as shares or bonds, then this must always take place over Fiat currencies. At present one cannot exchange an Apple share for example directly into a Microsoft share. This only works over exchanges via USD etc., and thus additional fees are always due. Furthermore, the corresponding trading places are intransparent, because only the stock exchange operator or the stock exchange supervisory authority has insight into the actual transactions.

Solution explanation: Blockchains could solve both: by displaying shares or bonds as tokens on a blockchain, transactions become not only more transparent, but also interoperable, as is the case with cryptocurrencies. Different blockchains follow similar cryptographic algorithms. For example, the tokenization of physical values could create unprecedented compatibility and thus liquidity. A share token on the blockchain can thus easily be exchanged for another share token without the need for an intermediate fiat currency.

Challenges: As with all decentralized systems, the main challenges are speed, scalability and the associated problems. On a stock exchange such as Frankfurt or New York, thousands of shares are bought and sold every second. They could be transferred immediately via a centralized system. With a decentralized system, this does not work quite so easily because the centralized organizational partner does not exist. Furthermore, it has been shown that decentralized systems always tend towards centralization due to efficiency mechanisms. You can see this in mining or in liquidity. This would probably not result in a large number of different trading pairs, but mainly those with the most liquidity - such as fiat money as the trading currency.

Alternative possibilities: This raises the relevant question how far a completely decentralized tokenization will be released here at all. Perhaps it needs more transparency than compatibility. The former could also be guaranteed by centralized systems. Therefore, this area of application is not necessarily predestined for a blockchain.

Practical examples: Nevertheless, trading venues and exchanges should take a close look at decentralized systems, as they may one day be completely replaced by such decentralized exchanges. NASDAQ in the US, for example, has also been testing a potential application for some time now, and I expect there will be a few more to follow.

COMPANY REGISTRY
(COMMERCIAL REGISTRY ...)

Problem description: One could classify company registries similar to that of securities or to the land registry. There is the problem of the transparent and unchangeable presentation of company property. Just as with land, legal certainty would be important for investments on the one hand, but on the other hand a cheaper and simpler alternative seems necessary to registry companies. In some countries, for example, it is extremely expensive and complicated to set up a LLC. Not because this procedure itself is so complicated, but because the administrative procedures are sometimes so lengthy and frustrating.

Solution explanation: A blockchain can help here decentrally, because it represents ownership which is unchangeable and transparent. At the same time, this tokenization would be optimal for interoperability with other blockchains. Registering a company on a blockchain could then cost a small update fee of just a few USD or crypto coins - goodbye to administrative formalities and bureaucracy!

Challenges: The challenges here are to revolutionize established bureaucratic processes. However, this is much easier said than done at many public offices. What is needed above all is legal acceptance of the fact that a token on a blockchain actually represents a proportion of the company. For example, I am often asked when security tokens could become equity tokens, i.e. when tokens can reflect company shares in an ICO. This has nothing to do with the blockchain per se, but the conversion only works if regulators offer a legally binding possibility that a token can really represent a company property. When this will happen is still quite unclear in most countries today.

Alternative possibilities: There are plenty of centralized alternatives. Countries like Estonia now offer fully automated company registrations on the Internet at incredibly favorable conditions. If you pair this with an e-Identity, you get a centralized but incredibly efficient system, which could question the need for a decentralized blockchain.

Practical examples: You can register your company on the blockchain in addition to a normal company registration. Of course, this decentralized registration is not legally binding. Some Baltic states are even testing blockchain solutions in this area. The state of Delaware in the USA, which is known for simple company registrations, also wants to offer company registrations on the blockchain. So I hope that such solutions will soon set a precedent worldwide.

I can only advise every employee or official in the public service to take a close look at such applications in order to be able to offer bureaucracy-free and trustless solution models. States live off their companies - so if you want to lure them into your own country, you need attractive offers. This would be such a thing.

REAL ESTATE (APARTMENTS, REITS …)

Problem description: Real estate brings with it similar problems to many of the assets we have already discussed. So I am not going to go into things like transparency and ownership as they apply here as well. I am referring at this point to the problem of the enormous costs involved in buying and selling real estate. These fees often account for more than 10 percent of a total property purchase and arise from registration fees (about 3.5 percent), stamp duties (about 1 percent), notary fees (about 1 percent), brokerage fees (3 to 5 percent) and some other fees. All these fees would be reduced to a minimum if registration, transfer and guarantees were easier to handle.

Solution explanation: Registering real estate on a blockchain could easily solve this problem. Since they can be easily linked to their blockchains, the transfer and registration is fast, easy, smooth and transparent. Smart contracts could eliminate fiduciary fees, and through better insight and transparency, there would be greater liquidity, which would significantly reduce brokerage fees, as it would be easier to find suitable properties. Exactly the same happened with shares a few decades ago, when they were made liquid on an electronic stock exchange for the first time without stock traders. While previously there was a transfer fee of 10 percent in some cases, most online brokers have reduced these fees to less than 1 percent because they no longer needed people to trade. As soon as real estate is displayed liquidly and transparently via blockchains and linked to each other, the same would happen.

Challenges: The challenges lie mainly in the slow bureaucratic system, which would rather continue to charge high fees for inefficiency than drive efficiency forward. Many of the parties involved in real estate holding out their hands do not want the technology to improve. They would lose their livelihood as a result. I can understand part of that, but one will always drive innovation forward. When the time comes, it's better to be prepared rather than just running after and losing market share.

Alternative possibilities: That fees in the real estate market will fall is practically guaranteed. This is already seen as a consequence of online platforms that have emerged in recent years. Whether such solutions will continue to be centralized or decentralized at some point, however, is far from certain. Decentralized solutions would have some interesting application examples nonetheless.

Practical examples: Implementations in this area are similar to those in the land registry or company registry. Due to the tokenization of physical assets, larger investments could be shared more easily, so that smaller investors would also have access to them. REITs are already doing this on a centralized basis. However, decentralized tokens could be exchanged completely smoothly with other values. Blockchains would provide way more flexible use of capital and through intraoperability would therefore drive additional liquidity into the market.

Of course, there will always be setbacks. In a pilot project in this area it happened through a bug (mistake) that several real estate users lost their real estate on the blockchain. Most real estate blockchains are not too fast because transactions do not have to be done in milliseconds. Therefore, it takes a few days until these are effectively set on the blockchain. In this case, an otherwise extremely rare reversal occurred after a few days. The participants knew that they had to wait at least one week until they had to consider a transaction of more than 10,000 USD as fixed. But in this case this was disregarded. The real estate was first bought; then however the purchase was reversed falsely again. The buyers would have had to bear the whole costs themselves. Since it concerned however only a pilot project, the damage was taken over by the initiator. This again showed how important it is to think through different scenarios carefully, especially with new technologies, so that a great idea does not lead to a bad implementation.

PRECIOUS METALS (GOLD, SILVER ...)

Problem description: Precious metals such as gold, silver or platinum bring with them a few other problems compared to goodwill or real estate. The main issues here are storage and liquidity. While many people hold gold, only very few have ever used it in their lives. Virtually no shop in the world accepts gold as a means of payment without further conversion.

Solution explanation: Friends of mine in Singapore and a few other companies worldwide offer solutions here. They replicate an ounce of gold over numerous stations and create a gold token on the blockchain as soon as the ounce has been safely stored in an independent safe. Gold is tokenized in this way and can be traded easily via stock exchanges. Of course, you have to trust the safe operator. However, since these are mostly certified institutions, the risk here is the same as if you were to store an ounce of physical gold yourself.

Challenges: Nevertheless, such solutions are not really decentralized, and some questions always remain unanswered: What if the gold is stolen from the safe? What if I lose my private key? So I'm not 100% sure myself whether such decentralized tokenization solutions will ultimately prevail for precious metals.

Alternative possibilities: There is also the option of storing gold in a single place and still issuing the equivalent value as a digital but centralized credit. Some companies and banks offer this option already.

Practical examples: Blockchains are definitely innovative here, but you always have to ask yourself which problem you want to solve and what would be the best solution. Personally, I wouldn't invest my time in this subset of blockchain applications.

BLOCKCHAIN APPLICATION 5: TRANSPARENCY

Since each blockchain participant can see the complete update history of the community, complete authenticity develops. As you will see right away, this area of blockchains is currently the most promising from my point of view. Personally, I believe that we will see an enormous number of the next blockchain applications from the ones listed here.

ACCOUNTING (INVENTORY, TAX CONSULTANT ...)

Problem description: Accounting serves the documentation of incomes and expenditures in the financial range, and can serve similarly as an admission of the current inventory. This area needs incredible resources in every company. Either the bookkeeping is done within the company itself, or it is outsourced to a tax office. This is only necessary because, from the outside, no one can ensure that the figures given by the company are correct. Trust that exists within a group cannot simply be conveyed to the outside world.

Solution explanation: A blockchain would be an extremely cost effective and simple solution. Regardless of whether it's about finances in accounting or objects in inventory: all updates can be displayed transparently on the blockchain, including timestamps. The signatures of the private keys can be used to irrevocably trace who took what and when. This can then be given either always or only by a „permission key" for inspection by a control authority. The involvement of a tax office or an auditor becomes obsolete.

Challenges: As already mentioned at the beginning of this chapter, I see almost all transparency blockchains as the next big blockchain category right after finance (cryptocurrencies) and smart contracts (Ethereum) due to their simple implementation. Problems are only caused by sluggish companies that do not invest in innovation. However, this will be resolved relatively quickly, because as soon as even a single company invests time and energy in this area, others will have to follow suit.

Alternative possibilities: My positive attitude towards this application area comes from the fact that I see relatively few alternative possibilities to a blockchain. Even other decentralized systems like the Tangle or a Hashgraph don't work optimally due to the missing ledger. Therefore I could imagine that this blockchain application will be one of the first to solve a clear and irrefutable problem. Of course, cryptocurrencies and smart contracts also solve problems, but with the transparency blockchains the existing problem is even more tangible.

Practical examples: There is a reason that IBM is investing an incredible amount of money here with the Hyperledger project and is pushing this area enormously forward. Every accounting firm, tax office and inventory taker has to inform themselves as quickly as possible in order to stay up to date. If you are an employee in such a company, then draw the attention of your boss or educate yourself by informing yourself online. Contact our team for further help in this field: team@julianhosp.com

AUDITS (ISO-CERTIFICATIONS...)

Problem description: An audit is an inspection of a process by an outside independent company. The Big 4 have established themselves worldwide. This refers to the four large auditing companies Deloitte, Pricewaterhouse Coopers, KPMG, and Ernst & Young, and in many areas of business today it is state of the art to have your own statements confirmed by one of these four companies. This of course costs money, and once again trust in a centralized party is necessary.

Solution explanation: Processing via a blockchain would be extremely simple here, similar to accounting. Instead of documenting income and expenses on a blockchain, processes for an audit blockchain are logged decentrally and transparently with timestamps. In order not to carry business secrets to the outside world, these could be masked by the use of certain keys. Only those who have the relevant key have access to the data. If you do not have this key, everything remains secret for you. You can thus substantiate your own statements through the same process as in an audit by a renowned auditing company, except that you no longer need any money. The processes had to be logged anyway, but this happens now on a blockchain.

Challenges: The challenges here are more in the economic sphere. Many management consultancies strongly advise their companies against using blockchains for verifications, as this would be their own downfall. This behavior on the part of auditors somewhat inhibits innovation in this area. From a technical point of view, most of the systems could already be used.

Alternative possibilities: I don't really see any alternatives, because technological and economic progress can only be slowed down to a limited extent.

Practical examples: Since I am often booked as a consultant and speaker for the Big 4, I know first-hand that the big players are currently undergoing a major rethink. Instead of blocking blockchains, the audit providers are considering how they can offer them themselves as a solution. From my point of view this is an excellent and target-oriented step. IBM and some other companies are also investing a lot of capital here. Every company which is currently paid for audits, etc., must quickly reorient itself in order not to become misleading. Of course, this will also be exciting for ISO standards.

LOGISTICS (SUPPLY CHAIN, SHIPPING...)

Problem description: If you extend the scope of the audits to the tracking of goods all over the world, you get to the logistics blockchains. These are simple questions, for example: How can you ensure without trust that a supply chain has been adhered to? How can you trace a transport without trust? Where does the food really come from?

Solution explanation: The solution is similar to that for bookkeeping or identity: a product or object gets a clearly assigned ID on the blockchain, and numerous independent parties sign it when they use it in action. Timestamps can thus be used to clearly document when something is passing where and by whom. Of course it can still come to fraud. Since the signers automatically gain reputation the more successful objects they have already signed, they are punished for cheating by depriving them of their reputation.

Challenges: The challenge here lies in starting such a system. In order for the signers to act really independently, numerous participants are required, each of whom signs only a small partial step. Developing solutions for this still takes a little time. But I believe, as already mentioned in the previous chapter, that this type of blockchain will represent the next large decentralized applications.

Alternative possibilities: If you try to solve something like this centrally, there are always long-term conflicts of interest. Therefore, as with accounting blockchains, I see only a few alternatives to this solution here.

Practical examples: We have already discussed these ideas many times, and you should definitely consider how this could be implemented in your company. There are unlimited application possibilities here, such as supply chains or proof of origin for pharmaceutical products. I would like to discuss some of them in more detail in the following chapters.

GEMSTONES (DIAMONDS...)

Problem description: Being able to trace gemstones like diamonds back to the mine where they were mined would massively devalue illegally traded stones and blood diamonds and hopefully quickly put an end to the associated dirty business. Due to numerous bribes, it has never really been possible to create confidence in whether a stone is „dirty" or „pure" with the help of centralized systems.

Solution explanation: The solution would be a diamond blockchain in which the respective stone passes through different stations. Different partial steps are confirmed independently and transparently by timestamps. For example, first the mine, then a local certification company, then the country of origin, then the transport company, then an independent organization, an export company, an import company and another diamond dealer in their own country could each sign a diamond. In this way, research on a particular gemstone is much easier and more transparent to handle. In the case of resale, the new buyer can then also follow the entire history of the diamond in question through the blockchain without having to trust anyone.

Challenges: The real challenges in implementing something like this are not of a technical nature. Of course, there is still the danger of fraud if the different signers join forces and document the untruth in the blockchain. However, the risk is much better distributed here than with the current centralized variant, where a certificate, which can easily be falsified, has to take over everything. In reality, it is the lack of motivation of many participants that has prevented the successful introduction of a diamond blockchain so far. Many of the fraudulent participants involved in the diamond trade are under the same roof. They do not want the diamond trade to become more transparent. Many organizations are trying to break up this fraudulent cartel, but the billion-dollar gemstone industry is not making it that easy.

Alternative possibilities: From a logistics point of view, I don't see any alternatives as a blockchain to make the diamond trade more transparent. However, if artificial diamonds become more and more popular, they could solve the problem of the origin of the right diamonds in a different way. There would be enormous price pressure, forcing mines and diamond companies to raise their standards. Hopefully, then, the often bloody diamond business will be taken to task from several sides at the same time.

Practical examples: A diamond blockchain was one of the first applications I saw myself in 2014. But the true breakthrough has not really happened until today due to the numerous challenges. Perhaps you have the decisive idea for success here? This would not only be relevant for diamonds or other gemstones but could probably be transferred to many blockchain applications in general.

PHARMACEUTICALS (MEDICATIONS, DRUGS)

Problem description: What is relevant for gemstones is also essential in areas such as the pharmaceutical industry: Which ingredients were used for a drug? Where was everything manufactured? When was a drug produced? Especially today, when medicines are manufactured globally and shipped all over the world, such questions are essential when it comes to our health.

Solution explanation: Blockchains would be the ideal solution for listing the ingredients and dosage forms of drugs. It doesn't need one blockchain for everything, but there could be many small, different ones interacting with each other. Transparency and trust would achieve unprecedented values. This would also allow regions around the world to score points in terms of quality and price, from which consumers as of today may not dare to buy.

Challenges: As I have mentioned before, I see incredible application potential in logistics blockchains. That's why I think it's a pity that there are only a few entrepreneurs who deal with this area.

Alternative possibilities: There are practically no alternative possibilities, and that's exactly why I hope that you think about what you can transparently put on a blockchain here.

Practical examples: In the pharmaceutical sector there is the possibility to use blockchains for illegal drugs in addition to pharmaceutical drugs. This would then be a partially illegal application, but if you look at how much damage is usually caused not by the drugs themselves, but by toxic additives or by splashing and stretching of the originally pure substance, I would like to at least mention the possibility of transparent drug tracking here, even if this would be a partially illegal blockchain application. Such an application would make it quite simply possible to distinguish medically prescribed drugs from illegal drugs and at the same time maintain high quality standards.

COPYRIGHT PROTECTION (MUSIC, MOVIES, PROGRAMS, ROYALTIES, DIGITAL UNIQUENESS...)

Problem description: We have already discussed a similar blockchain application for patent and trademark protection in the ownership chapter. However, this is about how copy protection can be managed transparently and authentically and how artists or authors can be correctly rewarded for the use of their work at the same time. Licenses and royalties are such a hated topic among musicians because the singers do not know exactly how much they should receive. In addition, they have to give an enormous amount of the actual income to companies that control the music market.

Solution explanation: A blockchain could easily present copy protection, licenses and royalties in a transparent way and, due to its interoperability, could even solve them in a particularly cost-efficient way.

Challenges: The music market, like many other markets, is controlled by only a few large labels. Of course, they have no interest in giving up their power. Since most music is distributed digitally today, this application would actually be predestined for a blockchain.

Alternative possibilities: There are alternatives to a blockchain only in so far as the current music companies make the revenues available to their artists and originators in a more centralized, transparent and cost-effective way.

Practical examples: Of course, this is not only relevant to music. Films, computer programs, games and much more could also benefit enormously from such a blockchain solution. So just think a little bit for yourself, find a good niche and find a revolutionary solution in the relevant area.

ELECTIONS
(ELECTORAL SYSTEMS, REFERENDA)

Problem description: Whether it is a question of electing a president or a parliament, or voting for a specific political line in a referendum: when considering the trust side, voting is an extremely one-sided process. Those who set up and conduct the election have practically complete control. It is no wonder today that there is practically no election that does not speak of election fraud. This happens in industrialized countries just as it does in third world countries. Millions of USD and many working hours have to be invested beforehand and afterwards in order to prevent such electoral fraud or at least to uncover it afterwards. Most electoral systems with voting cards etc. are comparatively primitive, but so far only very few states have dared to digitize elections. This is due to an even greater confidence problem: what if the system were hacked? What if an error were to occur? How can anonymization be guaranteed? etc. I am sure that when you read these questions you immediately think of blockchain: trust, anonymization, etc. are classic topics of a decentralized blockchain.

Solution explanation: I think there is almost no problem that could benefit even more from a blockchain solution today than the holding of elections and referendums. An election blockchain could be set up 100 percent anonymously for all participants. Every eligible voter could use his private key to sign who he wants to vote for or what he wants to vote for via the blockchain. The election or referendum would be completely transparent, and this transparency could optionally only be established at a certain point in time, so that the voters themselves would not be influenced by the prior knowledge of how other voters voted. Each participant could support the blockchain itself, so the system would be completely decentralized. Since it would not be a calculation-intensive blockchain, it could even be displayed on a smartphone. In countries where people are threatened when voting, they could vote from home. Nobody could cheat on the system because it is protected by cryptography. Electoral fraud, miscounts, etc. would therefore be absolutely impossible.

Challenges: So what has kept governments from offering voting via a blockchain so far? The challenges to conduct elections via a blockchain are manifold but have almost nothing to do directly with blockchain technology. On the one hand, of course, there are political backgrounds: countries where electoral corruption is the order of the day do not want to give up power by creating systems that could overthrow those in power. But there are other challenges which are more logistical in nature and which we have already mentioned a few times: How can a voter clearly verify himself against the blockchain? How does a voter get his or her key? How is it prevented that people are not bribed in such an anonymous system? There are still no definitive answers to most questions today, as there are to their applications, which would come into question for a blockchain implementation.

Alternative possibilities: I can't think of a good alternative if you want to achieve fairness between voters and elected representatives. In order to overcome the problems, a mix of the current system and a blockchain would be the best solution today: People still have to go to a polling station, have to identify themselves there by passport or identity card, get a randomly generated key and dial in a locked cabin by blockchain. Even if the private key were fake, the blockchain could be set in such a way that once the vote has been taken, the decision can no longer be changed. One could then always ensure one's own private key that one's own voice would also be correctly noted on the blockchain. As long as no one else has the private key of other voters, no one can see their voting decision. Consequently, everyone sees the votes anonymously, but the individual votes cannot be assigned to individual persons. There are therefore possible interim solutions, which would only have to be implemented.

Practical examples: Enough pressure from the population, which would benefit enormously from this blockchain application, could lead governments to try out this system at least on a trial basis. Switzerland, which has an enormous number of direct referendums, is planning to offer such a pilot project. I am making a call to all governments or regulators: if you really want the best for your citizens, then you have to stay true to your word and use this great technology. I hope that you, as citizens, will take every opportunity to demand this from your country, so that the countries not only can do this optionally, but will soon also have to. It would be to the advantage of all of us.

ENERGY (ELECTRICITY SUPPLY, ...)

Problem description: In most countries, the electricity supply is practically monopolized. Few companies dominate the entire market. This results in poor and intransparent prices for customers. How could this be improved?

Solution explanation: One of the possibilities would be to transparently present supply and demand via a blockchain. Since more and more citizens are producing electricity themselves via solar systems, a fair market could be created in this way via a decentralized network, which would ultimately benefit everyone (except the large electricity suppliers).

Challenges: To represent current via a blockchain is obvious, because current is nothing else than wandering electrons, which can easily be captured in digitized form. Many of the problems that other applications have with environmental interaction are therefore eliminated here. A decentralized current blockchain is prevented primarily by all those who would be on the losing side by such a solution: the current monopolists. In order to overpower them (in the truest sense of the word), a cooperation between government and innovative companies is probably necessary, which can provide turnkey solutions. However, this will not be as simple as some startups in this field imagine. Because energy suppliers have a strong lobby and good relations to the top. They use all means to prevent decentralized electricity platforms.

Alternative possibilities: There is also still the possibility of centralized transparency. Instead of a blockchain, energy suppliers offer a transparent but centralized trading platform. Some are already doing that. This might be easier to achieve and would make a blockchain solution unnecessary for the time being.

Practical examples: The easiest way would of course be for one of the large corporations to go ahead and offer a decentralized solution. However, this would be a moonshot that would either go completely backwards or let the company survive as the only one. Therefore, electricity and energy on the blockchain have huge potential, only that the right catalyst is needed, especially from the political side (a hint to all politicians reading this book).

TRAFFIC IMPROVEMENT (TOLL BOOTHS, AVOIDANCE OF TRAFFIC JAMS)

Problem description: A traffic jam is one of the most annoying things for many people. Toll stations are often built to create so-called express roads, which can be used by paying extra. The avoidance of traffic jams could always be better achieved.

Solution explanation: Drivers could communicate with each other via a decentralized system. All those who want to drive faster could pay for all those who are content with slower progress. This reward and punishment system could of course be extended to many other things such as the health system or CO_2 emissions. All those who want to use a resource more or faster pay as punishment a compensation to those people who make less use of this resource. A blockchain could handle all this decentrally and transparently.

Challenges: The current systems are usually controlled by large corporations or governments, which slows down and complicates any change.

Alternative possibilities: Furthermore, centralized systems of course could also be considered as an alternative.

Practical examples: However, such possibilities would once again enable anyone to offer creative solutions that could then compete efficiently with existing methods. This could help many affected people.

DONATIONS (CHARITIES, FUNDRAISING)

Problem description: Have you ever given up donating because you were unsure what the charity would do with your money? This question always arises: will the recipient use the money as promised, or will he spend it elsewhere? Wouldn't it be great if the respective organizations could present money flows completely transparently? Every supporter would then know 100 percent that what he has donated money for has also arrived there.

Solution explanation: A blockchain can make exactly this transparent. I don't think I need to go into the details anymore. If you have already looked at the accounting, audit etc. applications, you should already be quite clear how to implement the whole thing.

Challenges: The challenges here are only in doing. Of course, it will not be possible at the beginning to present everything completely transparent, because for expenses of a donation organization via the blockchain its counterparty must also use a blockchain. This may not be the case for all partners at the beginning. But in the course of time an enormous pressure could arise for organizations to present their own processes in a transparent way as well.

Alternative possibilities: I don't know of any alternative solutions where you don't need a third party. Go, go, blockchain!

Practical examples: Some charities are already grasping their way forward step by step. If you yourself operate such a charity or are active in such a charity, you should definitely take this path of transparency. It will pay off in the long term.

TAXES (GOVERNMENTS)

Problem description: Who likes to pay taxes? Nobody, I think. But if we are honest, every state needs an income, in the end it also takes care of us. Personally, I think that we are reluctant to pay taxes (among other things) because there is a lack of transparency. We simply don't know what the government does with the money it collects. It is true that the government lays down an annual budget, but in my opinion it would be much better if every single issue could be traced.

Solution explanation: As with donations, startup investments, sponsoring, etc., a state should - no, would have to! - use a blockchain here. In order to still be able to guarantee privacy for employees or a certain degree of confidentiality for certain projects, simply an intransparent sub-blockchain would be the right solution. With this solution, an outsider can see how much money has been spent in total by a certain authority or has flowed into a certain project, but the exact distribution remains invisible. This would allow essential details, such as strategic military expenditure or the salary of a non-politically exposed person, to be kept secret.

Challenges: Once again, the challenge is not of a technical nature, but rather due to the reluctance of individual states. Those in power do not want the state to be 100 percent transparent. Nor do they want to answer the citizens' questions about every issue. In the beginning there would certainly be a loud outcry by the population, if suddenly many of the expenditures, which were mixed with others before, were completely transparent and clear.

Alternative possibilities: If a state really wants to create transparency and trust, there is no way around a blockchain. It would not even have to be completely decentralized. Especially at the beginning, only a few things need to be transparent, and in the course of time this visibility for the population could be extended.

Practical examples: Unfortunately, there are still no states that are making progress here. However, this solution would create enormous added value for its population. So I hope that the day will come when it will no longer be accepted if a state denounces the blockchain solution. Many things that were also unthinkable a few decades ago are perfectly normal today. I wish the same for these improvements as well. My father always said: „Son, wishes are allowed". Well hopefully father state listens here also!

DECENTRALIZED AUTONOMOUS GOVERNMENTS (STATES ON THE BLOCKCHAIN)

Problem description: When we talk about states and blockchains, we finally come to an essential question: can an entire state be brought onto a blockchain? What problems would this solve? In principle, such a blockchain would distribute the entire trust that citizens place in a state among the citizens themselves. Many of the applications such as identification, land registry, taxes, etc. would be included. Many dropouts, who are already giving back their passports and citizenship in order to live on an island without taxes, are trying to take such a path. So would it be possible to actually map an entire state on a blockchain in order to decentralize trust in this way?

Solution explanation: Some states, especially in the South Pacific and the Caribbean, are making initial attempts to approach such a solution. A blockchain would really make all information, laws, decisions and changes transparent and unchangeable for everyone. The entire bureaucracy could be reduced to a minimum. Administrative acts would be taken over by smart contracts, decisions taken every day by all citizens. That would be democracy at the highest level.

Challenges: But is this really a good solution? Of course, the advantages of a blockchain are obvious. But so are the disadvantages. For example, the following questions would have to be decided equally by an entire population: Should a state go to war? How high should the taxes be? Such a system would be incredibly rigid, and with each participant a new opinion would probably be added. In my opinion, such a system would resemble an anarchy rather than any other form of government.

Alternative possibilities: There is certainly much that can be improved on today's governments. But I personally believe that this task must be subdivided. There is nothing like a Jack of all Trades that can do everything. If you want decentralization and a reduction in power, this in turn limits agility. In my opinion, more attractive alternatives will come from centralized organizations, even if I personally would prefer a decentralized solution. But I could imagine, for example, that Facebook or Google could create a „Planet Earth" country - a digital country with its own passport, rights and everything that makes citizenship. Even if all this sounds partly dystopic, I can imagine something like this rather than a completely decentralized organization as a state.

Practical examples: Nevertheless, Puerto Rico is trying to establish itself as a separate blockchain country within the framework of a project. There are very few details on this, but maybe if you read this book sometime in the distant future, you can apply for a passport as a „Blockchainian".

DECENTRALIZED AUTONOMOUS ORGANISATIONS (FRANCHISE COMPANIES)

Problem description: When looking at smaller organizations below the state level, the question also arises whether they can be decentralized as a community. Relatively quickly, possibilities open up to bring justice, trust and transparency to a group through blockchain technology. Since this would eliminate organizational effort, possible maintenance costs could be extremely reduced at the same time.

Solution explanation: We have already discussed

blockchain-based organizations in general on a number of occasions, but here I would like to give a few special examples which might be of interest for you. There will be an incredible number of other possibilities here, especially if people are no longer directly involved in maintaining the organization. The decentralized financing, the lack of costs or the renunciation of decisions that have to be made explicitly by people, leads to unbelievably high returns. Therefore I am of the opinion such decentralized autonomous organizations (DAOs) can revolutionize many enterprise structures, as soon as more robots and machines are used in the operation.

Here are few examples:

- A self-driving car is registered as DAO, administrates itself autonomously and pays dividends to the token holders of the car.
- Franchise enterprises or hotels that are completely managed by robots can come up. There are already some test objects active, where no humans can be found anymore but only robots. Here a DAO can be set up that is funded by humans und pays them dividends.
- Even self-service super markets are possible with that solution, similar to those by Amazon in America.

Challenges: The initial difficulty with such DAOs is

certainly the lack of acceptance by the population. But acceptance will come as soon as people get used to be surrounded only by robots for some things. What then could prevent these decentralized organizations from succeeding? The decentralized organization itself! The very first Decentralized Autonomous Organization was established as „the DAO" in 2016 on the Ethereum blockchain as an investment vehicle. The aim was to create a decentralized investment fund in which people could invest and vote on their investments via an algorithm. Since the DAO had no management, because this task was taken over by the blockchain, there were practically no costs, and 100 percent of the investment profit could have been paid out to investors. Within a few weeks, almost 150 million USD were invested in the DAO. However, it turned out shortly thereafter that a hacker had found a bug (fault) which enabled him to get the DAO to send him almost 60 million USD. The question was always whether this was a bug or a feature. Had the beneficiary of these shares really cheated, or had he simply exploited the publicly available rules in his favor? The DAO code, just like a public contract, was open source and therefore readable for everyone. Most had just not read it - with the exception of the „hacker". Is it now illegal to exploit clearly stated rules, even if this may not have been in the inventor's interest?

Who defines exactly what the original idea was? Lawyers all over the world are paid every day to find loopholes in contracts and to exploit them for the benefit of clients. Are these people therefore criminals? Shouldn't one then see a person who has exploited a digital contract in his favor in the same way? Excitingly, legal experts really do not agree on this. It is still not clear whether the unknown person committed a crime in 2016 or not. The blockchain world, on the other hand, did something that had previously been considered impossible: it split Ethereum into a strand in which the hack had never taken place and one in which it had happened. This is how ETH and ETC came into being. To this day, it bears witness to how difficult it is to set up DAOs correctly.

The great difficulty of DAOs lies in the creation of rules. These rules must not only work at the time they are set up, but for an indefinite period of time beyond that. These smart rules, which we also learned about with cryptocurrencies, will be essential when it comes to allowing a self driving car, for example, to operate completely autonomously. How does this car adapt if, for example, cars are no longer allowed in a city? Does it drive into another city? Does it commit „suicide"? How does it adapt to new laws? Many questions that nobody can answer today.

Alternative possibilities: These challenges lead to the consideration of whether such things like self driving cars, franchises, etc. should simply remain centralized. This is possible, but I don't believe it. What is needed is a decisive breakthrough in the game theoretical design of smart rules.

Perhaps we simply need a bit of hierarchy here instead of complete decentralization. We will see practical examples.

Practical examples: In any case, DAOs are an incredibly exciting part of the blockchain world. Personally, I believe that much of what we invest in today can be managed as a Digital Autonomous Organization in the future. The profit then goes away from the companies that actually first did the work in question to those that establish DAOs with the same tasks. So maybe think about the conceivable use cases beyond the ones mentioned above and create your own DAO.

DECENTRALIZED AUTONOMOUS CORPORATIONS (NON-PROFIT ORGANISATIONS, TEAMS)

Problem description: DAOs inevitably lead to DACs, Decentralized Autonomous Companies. This is about making companies more efficient and transparent as a whole.

Solution explanation: In principle, DACs function exactly the same as DAGs or DAOs, they are only specialized in companies or teams. Depending on their orientation, such DACs can be profit-oriented or non-profit. According to the specific smart rules, such a DAC can implement different applications and work even more efficiently than a classic company as we know it today.

Challenges: The challenges are similar to DAOs. They just have to be much more agile than these. Anything that can't adapt quickly enough will disappear from the market.

Alternative possibilities: When considering alternative possibilities, you first have to consider whether DACs are really trying to solve a real problem. I don't believe that 100 percent of the time. From my point of view, there may not be any alternatives at all, since DACs may also be completely superfluous.

Practical examples: Unfortunately, DACs are often misused for fundraising by organizations through hype marketing. Theoretically teams, companies, non-profit etc. could profit from it. In reality, however, this is much more difficult to implement than in theory. However, in order to collect millions of USD through ICOs, a new hype term is invented with the sole aim of distinguishing itself from boring traditional investments. I am extremely skeptical about all the blockchain applications that have to adapt agilely to innovations, because what a blockchain is not, is easily changeable. DAGs, DACs and possibly DAOs once again show how important it is not simply to blindly jump on the blockchain hype, but to rationally question the meaningfulness of the individual solutions

REPUTATION (PERSONAL REPUTATION, PRODUCT QUALITY, CORPORATE IMAGE)

Problem description: We have often talked about the necessity of an identity on a blockchain. However, this is also linked to one's own reputation or the reputation of a company or its products. Warren Buffett said in a famous quote: „You need a lifetime to build your reputation, but only a few seconds to destroy it. If you remember that more often, you will approach decisions differently." I find the quote enormously inspiring and try to orient myself to it whenever possible. But it is often difficult to clearly outline the reputation of another person or company. All too often there are problems with fake identities or fake reputation. This not only affects people, but also food, medicines, branded products, etc. So how could fake be distinguished from non-fake? How could one prove over the Internet that one's reputation is rightly good?

Solution explanation: A logistics blockchain can be a solution, similar to the topic of identity. You could have a person's actions recorded by other people on the blockchain in order to get feedback on a person's actions in the course of time and build a reputation on them. All those who evaluate other people also receive a score through their actions. This creates a reputation system of the scorers and the people who are scored. Through the timestamps it would be incredibly difficult to cheat on such a blockchain. There would be an enormous value for all involved. If, for example, you interact with a person or a company for the first time, they can identify themselves via the blockchain. So you get a trust score from a stranger right at the beginning. After a long time of building up a reputation, as Warren Buffett describes, an ever-increasing value of a person or a company arises because the reputation improves more and more in the course of time. Nobody will want to destroy this hard-earned reputation through stupidity. Theoretically the reputation could even be expressed by a calculated monetary value. An algorithm could calculate a risk score that quantifies the probability that a counterparty would cheat for a certain sum or not.

Challenges: Of course, such a system raises almost more questions than answers. The biggest question that arises is that of the transparent human being. We have already talked about the Big Brother system in China in the identification chapter. Such a reputation system would only aggravate a class system of people. At some point nobody wants to interact with the people from the „lower" class anymore, because this could worsen their own reputation. As it is so often in the blockchain world, something sounds great in theory, but then fails not because of technology, but rather because of other reasons - as in this case social circumstances.

Alternative possibilities: Are there alternative possibilities? LinkedIn tries to build something similar using the existing centralized platform. Of course, a single company has full control here, and it's hard to extend the whole thing to other areas. Whether people really want to give up their privacy decentrally is more than just a legitimate question. That's why I don't believe that a worldwide reputation system can prevail. But perhaps you have the decisive idea, because if applied correctly, many problems could be solved by such a reputation blockchain.

Practical examples: Even though some startups are already devising solutions here, I consider them more than critical due to the potential control possibilities. I can imagine that people would like to know the reputation of other people. Less easily imaginable, however, is that they themselves want to reveal everything about themselves in return for participating in such a system. In my opinion, this conflict will make a blockchain solution in this area relatively difficult to implement, unless it remains focused on niches. A reputation blockchain would not only solve reputation issues worldwide, but similar to the Hashgraph technology, it could also solve some consensus issues in the decentralized world. For example, mining could be done through reputation rather than staking or work. The big discussion about wasting resources would then be solved once and for all. Furthermore, other blockchains could connect to the reputation blockchain and query information from it without trust. We will now discuss a few of these possible applications in detail in the next chapters.

FAKE NEWS
(NEWSPAPERS, SOCIAL MEDIA, BLOGS)

Problem description: The first niche for a reputation blockchain would be an application with the aim of preventing fake news. We all know the problem: on social media, in a blog or in a newspaper, lurid headlines on a topic are often spread. How do we know whether the article is correct or not? Maybe the medium only wants to do propaganda by forming wrong opinions? If one newspaper reports one thing and another newspaper the other, which of the two is correct? How can we prevent any bots on social media from spreading false news? Especially in the digital age, developments are not getting better, but worse and worse.

Solution explanation: Of course, companies like Facebook and Twitter are working on solutions. But a blockchain could be a cross-company and trustless alternative. As already described in the reputation chapter, authors, media companies or reporters could be evaluated using a scoring system, which would then be recorded on a blockchain with timestamps. Newspapers or social media platforms could then be forced to display the corresponding reputation score with every post or article. Authors gain reputation through articles or good content that prove to be true, authors lose their good reputation completely through lies. This should hopefully prevent authors from spreading false news, especially if their score was already very high before.

Challenges: The challenge hereby is that newspapers, media companies and social media providers need to join this system. The big question will be whether these giant corporations see any kind of incentive to participate. This can be but does not have to be. Furthermore, it has to be ensured that oracle systems evaluate as independently as possible, in order to ensure fair scoring. Here it must be prevented at all costs that fraud is committed, otherwise the whole system would be worthless.

Alternative possibilities: Media companies and newspapers could of course also simply create their own centralized systems and offer them through networking. The power of these companies must not be underestimated under any circumstances. It is doubtful whether they would voluntarily hand them over to a decentralized system.

Practical examples: I see that such scoring systems are guaranteed to come. A company that launches such a system is sufficient to put everyone else under pressure and follow suit. There will come a point where the consumers of the content will demand that a reputation score with the posted content will be clearly displayed. Whether this will happen via blockchains, however, will depend on whether companies in the media sector can arrange themselves centrally. Therefore, it will probably not be easy for a startup from the outside to gain a foothold in this field, which is only dominated by a few companies. Finally, Facebook could also create a blockchain itself. So the theoretical need for a blockchain is there in any case; whether it can ever be implemented in practice cannot be said with certainty from today's point of view.

EDUCATION SYSTEMS (SCHOOLS, TEACHING…)

Problem description: Another field in this category that could benefit from a higher quality standard would be school education. How can students' parents be sure that the content taught by a school is really correct? In most cases, teachers or professors do not intentionally teach their pupils or students incorrect content, but when this happens, the school materials are usually simply outdated or simply wrong. So how could students, parents, teachers or even states themselves ensure that the content is correct?

Solution explanation: A blockchain could again be used to record a reputation score for the books or other documents used. A global trustless database would be freely accessible to everyone and experiences could be shared among each other, which would benefit others.

Challenges: The challenges here are very similar to those of fake news or reputation blockchains in general. And there is an essential question to ask oneself: Is a blockchain at all necessary for something like this?

Alternative possibilities: I would strongly question the fact that the subject matter actually needs to be evaluated via a blockchain. That it should be evaluated, yes, that is actually a problem. But this could also be achieved much more efficiently via a centralized SQL database. With fake news there are too many different interests, therefore a blockchain could make sense there. But I strongly doubt whether the correct learning content has to be stored decentrally.

Practical examples: I know some startups in this area, but I believe that they use a blockchain because of a quick buck and not because of their greater utility. There is a real problem, but I think it should be solved in a centralized and not decentralized manner.

CURRICULA VITAE (CERTIFICATES, TESTIMONIES, UNIVERSITY DEGREES)

Problem description: Another challenge in the school system arises when you have finished school and are looking for a job. With every application you need a curriculum vitae that documents experiences, certificates and training.

BLOCKCHAIN APPLICATION 5: TRANSPARENCY

As an entrepreneur building up companies, I have hired new people almost every week. This means that I see dozens of CVs every day, where I have to be able to understand whether the statements on them are correct or not. We now have a person in the company who does nothing else than research whether the CV is factually accurate. Especially in times of globalization and digitalization this problem is getting bigger and bigger. Because applications come from all over the world, one must ask oneself, whether a course was actually completed or whether the certification was simply forged.

Solution explanation: This problem could be solved very easily with a blockchain: pupils and students record certificates, grades, diplomas and other results of their school career transparently on the blockchain with a time stamp. Instead of a CV, you send a potential employer a signature of the update history on the blockchain. In my opinion, this is an enormously elegant implementation of a reputation blockchain.

Challenges: Such an implementation really makes sense, because there are many different parties involved. A decentralized blockchain can handle this task pretty much as the only sensible solution. However, the widely dispersed geographical distribution of participants such as universities, schools and other educational institutions also poses a challenge. A standard is needed for the blockchain in question to ensure that everything is documented in a uniform manner.

This standard must first be established.

Alternative possibilities: The only alternative to this would be a centralized system like LinkedIn, which can also represent a kind of curriculum vitae via references and evaluations, which has been confirmed by other people. Nevertheless, I think a blockchain could be a better and more trustworthy solution to this problem.

Practical examples: Theoretically, each student could start his own blockchain business. It would even be very clever to start here in a niche and represent a single university or school on the blockchain. Maybe you could even start with just one subject. From there, the system would then be extended to other schools or universities until a comprehensive system exists. Later, such a system would be extended not only to the school system, but even beyond other advanced training courses and could perhaps even become an accepted reputation blockchain. Personally, I think it would be a big mistake to start here very broadly and generalized. One would have to get too many different parties and thus interests under one hat, which resembles a chicken-or-egg problem, where the one always waits for the initiative of the other.

RATING PLATFORMS (HOTELS, RESTAURANTS, FORUMS)

Problem description: I'm sure that whenever you go to a new restaurant or hotel, you've already looked at various online reviews. Maybe you have already given a rating yourself after a trip or a meal in order to warn others or to praise something especially. But how do we know if such feedback is fake or real? The same question arises at Amazon, for example, when customers rate products purchased there online. What is paid, fake feedback, and what is real? Especially in times of digitalization and e-commerce, the feedback of others can have a massive impact on one's own purchase. This is why there is so much power behind such rating platforms. So how could such a system be set up so that it cannot be manipulated by a single party, but is used transparently and fairly?

Solution explanation: You have already guessed it; the solution is a blockchain. This would work similar to a fake news blockchain, where past ratings would have more influence on new ratings. Because it's decentralized, it can't be abused by a single company for its own benefit.

Challenges: Such a blockchain would theoretically be a great solution for the problem described here. The big challenge is the acceptance by the existing platforms. Why should such a platform decentralize the feedback system via another network and not offer it itself, as it usually does anyway? This will be the crux of the matter when implementing such a blockchain in this field.

Alternative possibilities: As alternatives there are already feedback systems on almost all platforms, which are getting better and better. For example, if a user gives feedback and other people find it helpful, the value of a new feedback will increase in the future. Furthermore, reviewers can verify themselves and thus incorporate even more trustworthiness into a rating. Of course, the entire thing is still centralized. The operator of the platform, usually the retailer or service provider himself, whose products or services are evaluated, can censor, modify or even delete contributions in order to pursue potential financial interests with the help of the evaluations. In the end, nobody likes to cut off the branch they are sitting on.

Practical examples: In my opinion, the only way to start a blockchain in this area is to start in a niche. Online shops, travel platforms, feedback portals or other websites that benefit from feedback could be tackled in this way. Decentralized forums, such as a decentralized Reddit, could also be designed accordingly. Once an industry has been conquered, it can be scaled from there to other areas. In this way, this area will hopefully be used transparently and comprehensibly at some point.

DNS-ROUTING (INTERNET PROVIDER)

Problem description: To route information over the Internet, so-called routing tables are necessary. In these tables, DNS information is stored in a phonebook similar to addresses. One hears again and again about DNS hacks, with which attackers change the information in the tables.

What happens is they attract unsuspecting website visitors to a scam page instead of the page they actually want. There, credit card data or passwords are stolen from the visitors, which they then enter on the supposedly secure page. With this method, bank websites, credit card sites, social media sites or other financial platforms are regularly hacked, and users suffer millions in damages. If you want some more information look for „Julian Hosp DNS Hack".

Solution explanation: The solution to making these routing tables more transparent and to avoid hacks as much as possible would be to map the information to a blockchain. The application range for this would even be optimal, since every change of the tables can be designed in a comprehensible way. In this way, every node in the Internet can check at any time in a trustless manner whether it has saved the correct DNS address settings or not.

Challenges: Even if a blockchain would be a universal solution for this, in practice it is not possible to do this in the same way because the DNS routing tables are a very popular system. One would really have to change profound structures of the Internet here, which of course does not happen overnight. Many of the services based on DNS would then also have to be adapted, which only makes the entire thing more difficult.

Alternative possibilities: There are only limited alternative solutions, for example SSL certificates. Thus the question remains whether one is satisfied with the current solution or not.

Practical examples: Nevertheless, at least first tests with a blockchain could be performed. Someone who wants to offer a decentralized solution in this area needs a lot of experience in the field of Internet routing protocols and cryptography. On Ethereum, for example, there is the Ethereum Naming Service (ENS), which can store address data decentrally. This is still more of a proof of concept, but could easily be extended to general concepts.

BLOCKCHAIN APPLICATION 6: REDUNDANCY

Since everyone in a decentralized system stores everything from everyone, the redundancy of the data creates enormous security for the entire system.

Some of the applications in this chapter are self-explanatory and often build on other applications from the previous chapters.

Nevertheless, I find it important to treat the areas here again separately, as they underline the versatility of a blockchain. This is precisely where unique solutions for important problems often lie.

SWARM BEHAVIOUR (DRONES, NANOBOTS ...)

Problem description: I'm sure you've seen flocks of birds or schools of fish. The fascinating thing about sometimes thousands of living creatures moving in harmony is that nobody and everyone at the same time has the responsibility for the swarm as a new superorganism. The change of direction is carried out abruptly and apparently without error.

A good friend of mine is the founder of a drone show company. Maybe you've seen hundreds of little drones perform 3D shows in the air, live or on TV. It's really breathtaking! But the interesting thing is that they currently only coordinate a maximum of 500 different drones at the same time.

If one compares this with the abilities of animals to bring thousands of living beings into harmony at the same time, then the question arises why animals can do this, and we, the much more intelligent humans, cannot.

The reason is decentralization. In a flock of birds, not a single bird is the leader, but the group together sets the direction and the beat. The human being is more inclined to build centralized systems to control the whole from a single position because of his or her ability to lead. In the case of drones, for example, this means that the flight path of each individual drone is controlled by one central server. This centralization is easier to program, easier to understand and easier to maintain. But what if the server fails or the computing capacity is not sufficient? These limitations are also the reason why the company can only fly a few drones at the same time. If the system is overloaded and a server fails during a drone show, all drones fall on the audience. There is no redundancy per design. If there were no centralized server, but instead each drone would arrange itself decentrally just like a bird or fish in a swarm, perhaps a drone could have a problem in a worst case; the rest of them would not be affected. This problem does not only exist with drones, but everywhere where numerous objects should communicate with each other instead of being controlled from one single place. How can you learn from Mother Nature here?

Solution explanation: Banally speaking, nature uses an enormous number of possibilities for redundancy. Be it the swarming behavior of the animals or the DNA as a strand of basic building blocks of life. Nature always ensures that everything is protected twice and three times by numerous lanes, so that if something goes wrong, alternatives can take over. A blockchain could be used on drones and all other objects operating decentrally in the future, in order to establish such an emergency system. Drones then coordinate with each other when they need to be where. Objects such as small nanobots, for example, could be emitted in the billions. In the future, these small robots will be used in medicine to actively combat diseases in the body. In order to coordinate them, however, a decentralized rather than a centralized system will be necessary.

Challenges: The big challenge in such a system is the scaling, one of the weaknesses of each blockchain. So it may be that a hybrid solution of centralization and decentralization is needed to achieve the necessary speed of the system at millions or billions of participating units. Of course, technologies such as nanotechnology must first be developed to such an extent that blockchain can be used at all.

Alternative possibilities: In my opinion, the necessity of at least partial decentralization of these human swarm systems is based solely on one fact: as soon as a single error occurs in a centralized system, the call for more security and thus for a decentralized solution becomes very loud. However, the big discussion will be which of the decentralized systems are best suited for this purpose. This is impossible to predict from today's perspective, as there is still too little application experience. So you have to ask yourself with some blockchain startups in this area, if they have already paddled off too early for a wave, which will definitely come sometime. It may be decades before she really gets there.

Practical examples: The application possibilities in this field are enormous. For example, companies with drones, nanotechnology and many other applications are researching how to produce the required redundancy. Large corporations like Google see solutions for themselves here as well. If one wanted a blockchain startup here, one would definitely need experience in game theoretical swarm behavior, machine learning, cryptography and engineering. A subgroup, whose turn might be next, is that of the self-driving cars. We'll discuss this application next.

SELF-DRIVING CARS (TESLA, UBER)

Problem description: If one continues to spin the idea of keeping swarms, one comes to trustless solutions for self driving cars or even self-flying airplanes. One legitimate concern is what happens when a hacker takes control of such a car or aircraft. Then there will be no human in the vehicle to intervene.

Solution explanation: The solution is similar to that for drones. Instead of receiving commands from a centralized server, a self driving car must first update itself via a blockchain. Only when enough cars or airplanes have taken over a program, it will be implemented. So it's not enough to just update yourself, but as with a swarm, everyone else has to do the same. So it takes a bit longer until certain updates are adopted, but such a system would be much more resistant to hacking. If, for example, a car then recognizes that something is not correct in the program sequence in comparison to the others, its hard-coded system makes it move right and stop. Just as it is practically impossible to hack the health data of an individual user in a blockchain, it would also be incredibly difficult to hack a blockchain in self driving cars or airplanes.

Challenges: Of course, there are not only questions about the implementation of a blockchain, but one has to ask oneself in general if and when self driving cars or airplanes come. Some issues concerning liability in the event of accidents have not been finally resolved yet. At the same time, a dual system of centralization and decentralization will be needed at the very beginningl. The idea of giving up control has a completely different dimension here: it is linked to the question of who bears the responsibility in a system and therefore pays for potential damages.

Alternative possibilities: Even if self-driving cars are often coordinated centralized at the beginning, decentralized systems will definitely be used in the future. There are simply no alternatives to the necessary redundancy. Only the exact distribution between centralization and decentralization can be discussed.

Practical examples: This is precisely why companies such as Tesla, Uber, Google and all the other providers are researching such solutions themselves - not only in terms of the actual transport, but also in terms of increased security. If you are interested here, I can't necessarily recommend you to start your own business because of the high entry costs, but rather to work in one of the working groups of these large corporations.

You will not only learn there, but you will also be able to unfold much better due to the possibilities there.

INDESTRUCTIBLE DATA (INFORMATION RETENTION ...)

Problem description: Of course, digital redundancy can also be used simply to make data truly indestructible. Obtaining information for the future is essential for individuals, companies, and governments. For individuals, it will usually be sufficient to use corporate systems for this purpose. We've talked about this in other chapters. But as soon as it is a matter of securing the information of all mankind forever, you have to be creative. This is precisely why, for example, servers are built deep into the earth to protect information from potential meteorite impacts or other natural disasters. One of the reasons Elon Musk wants to go to Mars is to establish humans as a multiplanetary species with extra redundancy. How could this be effectively achieved?

Solution explanation: A blockchain would be an excellent application as long as you set up servers far enough distributed on the earth or theoretically also on the moon and other planets. The electricity required for this could be generated by solar modules. The corresponding servers would probably also hardly get any scaling problems, since you would only have to update the saved data once a day. If one server were to fail or be destroyed, this would have no effect on the others. The system would be an optimal safeguard. No question about it, it all sounds a little futuristic. But it is about preserving the legend of humanity forever - in my opinion every possibility should be used for this.

Challenges: Of course such a blockchain would be enormously expensive due to its size and geographical expansion. So there will be a lot of support from governments and other agencies needed to bring such a system to reality.

Alternative possibilities: Theoretically, such a system could also be set up centrally with distributed servers. The only problem is that if the centralized control unit fails, the system becomes unable to operate. This would not really secure such a system against a potential alien attack (yes, I believe in aliens) or meteorite impact. No matter if it's about this or other dystopian scenarios: I am convinced that a blockchain will prevail at some point.

Practical examples: Maybe reading this chapter, you'll think I've gone completely mad. I believe that visionaries should also deal with sometimes crazy games of thought, so that such ideas can be implemented later. In fact, there are already first attempts to create a decentralized interplanetary file system. How successful this will be, however, remains to be seen.

BLOCKCHAIN APPLICATION 6: REDUNDANCY

BIG DATA (GOOGLE, MACHINE LEARNING...)

Problem description: When we talk about indestructible data, the topics of big data and machine learning come up. What is big data? This involves extracting as much data as possible from a system in order to draw conclusions about the future. Whether it is Google, Facebook, Amazon or others, every company that deals with customers or products needs the ability to analyze data efficiently in order to survive economically. The big challenge at big data is therefore to reconstruct consumer behavior and use it economically. Here we are talking about the process of machine learning, for which computer algorithms are used. Where are the problems here to justify a potential blockchain application? On the one hand, big data requires privacy, a requirement that we have already discussed extensively. On the other hand, the same data set would need to be multiple and easily accessible so that machines can learn better from it. Right here blockchains could offer an advantage.

Solution explanation: Because data on a blockchain is displayed anonymously and redundantly on many servers simultaneously, big data and machine learning could benefit enormously from these decentralized systems.

Challenges: Data protection must be designed in such a way that consumers really remain anonymous. However, this cannot always be 100% guaranteed by recombination calculations with intentionally transparent blockchains. In a number of EU working groups in which I am a member, it is precisely this topic and possible proposed solutions, for example with regard to the basic data protection regulation, that are discussed. Another legitimate question is again the necessity of a blockchain to solve this problem. The problem is undoubtedly real, and so the solution lies in a blockchain. But is a blockchain really the most efficient and optimal solution?

Alternative possibilities: A perhaps significantly cheaper, faster and more efficient alternative would simply be a centralized controlled database distributed on different servers.

Practical examples: For exactly this reason I see many blockchain startups in the area of big data and machine learning as a good marketing gag rather than the most sensible implementation of a blockchain. Of course, it sounds better if you use several hype terms at once in a press article. This increases the chances of financial injections from public subsidies and private donors. If, however, the big players such as Google or Facebook are looking at this field, it can already be seen that they are clearly heading in the direction of centralized, highly efficient server systems and not towards blockchains.

BLOCKCHAIN APPLICATION 7: INCLUSIVENESS

Since a blockchain has no access controls and is not differentiated according to origin, age, gender, race, income, everyone and everything can join a blockchain by simply generating a private key.

I have already discussed this last field of inclusiveness with other applications. However, it is a really important aspect and one that gives blockchain solutions a unique advantage: the possibility that everyone can join a blockchain and never be excluded.

FREEDOM OF SPEECH (MEDIA, GOVERNMENTS)

Problem description: Censorship is ubiquitous. Be it governments, media or social media: we all know that those in power are willing to do almost anything to stay in power. Opinion-making is an essential tool of propaganda, and censorship is therefore an important instrument. Anyone who believes that this only happens in other countries, but not here, is far off the mark. Freedom of censorship is not just about not being able to block the newspaper article of a whistleblower, but rather about preserving an important good of mankind: the right to freedom of speech - whatever that may be.

Solution explanation: Whenever a system is centralized, censorship by definition is possible. That's why blockchain applications should always focus on being censorship resistant.

Challenges: We have already discussed the disadvantages of a blockchain in detail. Censorship resistance also means that harmful content such as child pornography, hatred or the glorification of violence can also reach the public uncontrolled. In a decentralized system there is no one who is in charge of what gets published. Thereby, the so called Werther effect can occur, named after Goethe's novel The Sorrows of Young Werther. In the novel, the protagonist takes his own life - and many readers of the novel followed suit. The Werther effect means that behavior that is normally rare suddenly leads to more imitators. This is conceivable not only for suicides, but also, for example, for amok-slaughters and the like. Freedom from censorship could only aggravate such problems. Something similar can already be seen in social media. Fewer and fewer people dare to express their opinions there because they perceive the sometimes negative reactions as part of social bullying. A system that is completely resistant to censorship could perhaps even lead to the complete opposite of what was originally desired. It is more likely to initiate a discussion of morality versus power than a question of technological implementation.

Alternative possibilities: As soon as a blockchain is not censored, it is by definition not decentralized. In such a case it must be asked whether a centralized system would not be better here.

Practical examples: This chapter is not so much about listing all applications again, but rather about emphasizing once again how important the ability to resist censorship is in a decentralized system. If you encounter areas in your environment where you would like less or no censorship, you should definitely consider using a blockchain. There are hardly any better applications than these and most of all media, governments and social media should consider technologically, socially and morally how they can use such systems efficiently for an added value of the population.

THIRD WORLD COUNTRIES (FINANCE, DEVELOPMENT AID...)

Problem description: One area where censorship resistance and inclusion are particularly important is the Third World. Again and again we hear that especially the poorest of the poor are denied access to the most essential things such as finances, identity documents, property and much more.

Solution explanation: Many people worldwide are working on solutions here. Blockchain would be one of them to enable inclusiveness. So if you really want to help the Third World, you should look at blockchain technology as a potential solution.

Challenges: Much more than mere access to a service, however, the countries and regions concerned often lack functional prerequisites. People who can read and write are often the exception, only very few have access to the Internet, smartphones are a luxury item, and perhaps only a few are allowed to use a computer in school. Often there is much more lack of training and implementation possibilities than of the actual technical prerequisites that a blockchain would need for success there. This brings us to the possible alternatives, which people often do not think about, who preach about blockchain applications in these areas of the world.

Alternative possibilities: There is no doubt that many centralized companies deliberately oppress people in developing countries. But do you really think they'll do that when alternative blockchain solutions come up? The sad scenario that I imagine here is that blockchains could trigger a revolution there, but that they would then be possible from centralized and much more efficient systems. Those who see this differently should ask themselves whether they can justify this rationally or whether they are not rather clinging to a utopian wishful thinking.

Practical examples: The problems described could also be the reason why there have been no real breakthroughs of blockchain startups in third world countries so far. Certainly there was good hype and good marketing and despite great hopes and numerous financing rounds so far no real results. Whether there will be such a thing at some point is still in the stars. Nevertheless, ideologically thinking people are necessary who hope for the best in the regions concerned and give everything they have to implement it. So if you want to help in third world countries, I can definitely advise you to consider blockchain technology as a tool. At the same time, the person concerned should not unconditionally expect to become the ultimate success. However, such an approach will ultimately force others to offer more humane and customer-friendly solutions not only to the First World, but everywhere else as well. For me, this would also be a success for the blockchain. It's not always about winning, sometimes it is more about adding value for everyone involved, whether through the technology itself or through its side effects.

REFUGEES (IDENTIFICATION, REGISTRATION)

Problem description: Only few refugees can directly help their precarious situation, in which they usually find themselves upon arrival in another country. Quite the opposite: most of them slide involuntarily into a situation in which they are without a home, money or identity card. Surely there are always black sheep, who exploit such situations maliciously. But the majority suffers without their own wrongdoing from exclusion from a society in which they will have to live more or less freely in the future.

Imagine what your life would look like without a bank account, smartphone or ID document. Furthermore, think about what possibilities for progress you would have at all. On one of my trips to Cuba I could see what such a situation can do to an entire country. In my life I had always been convinced that I would somehow manage to get out of any situation at any time and get to the top. When I saw the bad basic conditions there on the island, I doubted this conviction for the first time in my life. Even worse is the situation of a refugee. Not only that he does not possess anything anymore, but he also has practically no way of (re)obtaining the most essential basic building blocks, which would enable him or his family to make progress. Once a person gets into such a hopeless situation other instincts will be evoked, which might then be reflected in some of the problems of the refugee issue.

Solution explanation: Solutions must therefore start as early as possible. Of course, they cannot only be of technological nature. Nevertheless, I have mentioned many technical possibilities in the different blockchain applications, which could help enormously here. Once again, this chapter does not serve so much to repeat everything stupidly. Rather, it is a matter of examining some relevant social problems in order to consider how a blockchain could help to solve them. So definitely take a look at the chapters on identification, ownership and logistics again if you want to create added value for society here.

Challenges: The challenges of this work are similar to those of other blockchain applications when it comes to helping the poorest of the poor: different cultural and religious backgrounds, lack of education and lack of funding make it difficult to enter this technological advancement. This does not necessarily facilitate the already complex subject matter.

Alternative possibilities: States are also thinking about centralized possibilities. These could, of course, also be a technological solution. However, it will be important that they are interoperable. In addition, a solution should not only be available in a small region, but as widespread as possible. Open systems like a blockchain are much easier to use because everyone can contribute to the success, because no one has to rely on anyone else in such a system.

Practical examples: The refugee issue is therefore not only a social and ethical discussion in the media, but also a technological challenge. Most of the blows that have so far come from startups or governments have unfortunately not been much more than high-profile press releases. I personally have hardly seen any real implementations here yet. If this area is close to your heart, then step up! You would give the entire world an enormous amount of added value.

INTERNET OF THINGS (INDUSTRY 2.0, ROBOTS, SMART DEVICES, SMART HOMES)

Problem description: When we talk about participation in the future, it will not only be about people, but also about robots and machines. In addition to questions whether a machine has rights, whether it can be murdered by a machine or what a machine is legally allowed to do or not, there is also the question of how access to other possibilities for such machines is to be regulated. Especially when these are structured as independent or even as DAOs, one wonders: is there machine discrimination or is it not? What accesses are available to robots and machines? By and large, this is referred to as the Internet of Things (IoT). It's about the principle that in the future not only your laptop or mobile phone will be connected to the Internet, but pretty much any device. Communication between the individual devices is possible via access to the Internet. A toaster, for example, will be able to order his toast bread himself from Amazon Fresh. The toilet recognizes when the toilet paper is running low, then uses a smart shelf to check whether there is still a supply of toilet paper left and orders a new one if it is also used up. If these IoT-Devices have more and more possibilities, the following authorization is required with the question: can you trust them - and if so, how can that happen?

Solution: There is no question that such IoT devices will appear more frequently. Many large corporations produce, research and work on household appliances, vehicles or other products in that field. Together with other blockchain applications, these IoT devices could build a decentralized network among themselves, in which no single person or organization has control. This would significantly reduce the risk of hacking, increase trust and thus create added value for all.

Challenges: However, if no one has control over something, no one has the responsibility. We have addressed this challenge many times before. In IoT applications, it could have dramatic consequences if no one could intervene in a machine in the event of a malfunction. For example, what if a refrigerator suddenly started blackmailing its owner and deliberately bought something he was allergic to? In such cases, decentralization leads exactly to the opposite of what is desired. Experts agree that IoT devices could network with each other via blockchain. The challenges lie more in the potential consequences. Again and again there are a few funny missteps in the still young field of the blockchain. I kept one of these for you until the end: a company that developed a so-called smart thermostat wanted to design it through decentralization in such a way that nobody could manipulate it, not even the company itself. A user must verify himself correctly with the thermostat and adjust it manually so that it regulates the house temperature cleanly. All these rules were saved in advance. However, it was overlooked that there could be a potential hack attack on the thermostat system. The bug or the feature was exploited. A blackmailer set the thermostat to increase by one degree every hour until the homeowner paid a five-digit ransom sum to a crypto address. Nobody could reverse this hack, which underlines the advantages as well as the disadvantages of a decentralized system. The homeowners were thus gradually barbecued by the temperature control system, and the only solution was to destroy the thermostats with a hammer. I like to tell this anecdote because I want to remind you to be cautious, especially in such a young field where not all problems have been solved yet.

Alternative possibilities: Not only for the aforementioned reason I am not convinced that IoT really needs a blockchain. First, communication systems can be organized centrally, and second, I'm not quite sure if a single blockchain can connect all devices. Different systems may be required to communicate with each other. Such systems will probably be developed by the device manufacturers themselves and not by a single platform operator trying to solve everything. I certainly see the potential of blockchain solutions here, but I also see very good alternatives. As with the other blockchain applications, I believe in clear, specific implementations rather than in a king of all the trades, which is supposed to do everything.

Practical examples: I assume that in the future houses will becombined into smart homes, normal devices into smart devices and many other robots into IoT in order to communicate with each other. Even though highly innovative companies are researching a decentralized solution, I still believe that most of the processes will remain centralized for some time to come. With the catchwords Internet of Things and blockchain you can do great marketing today - but often there's not much behind it.

SPACE (SPACEX, NASA)

Problem description: This section deals again with a very futuristic topic: space. It is not so much a question of storing indestructible data, but rather of how to communicate over long distances and still keep information synchronous. Light, the fastest medium in the entire universe represents the time limit for our communication. From the earth to the moon it takes about 1 second. That's just a barely noticeable delay. But when it comes to distances to other planets, we're already talking about minutes and hours. If it's potentially even about communicating with other stars, we're equal to years. How do you prevent a potential attacker from modifying a system from starting to run asynchronously? Until one notices this and until one can react to it, much time passes and the backlog increases.

Solution explanation: With a blockchain, information could be kept synchronous over extremely long distances, without having to be afraid that an attacker might change something along the way. There is not one main station and many substations, but rather a data network where every station is equal. If you want to see this graphically represented in a short film, then go to YouTube and search for „Julian Hosp Mars blockchain". This is what space communication could look like in the long run.

Challenges: Keyword „could": the entire subject of space is still literally in the stars. Companies like SpaceX or organizations like NASA definitely have to make progress until potential applications of a blockchain in space become relevant at all. So go, Elon!

Alternative possibilities: Whenever a centralized party exists, this leads over long distances to massive deficits in the periphery. The Romans already established this a few thousand years ago, when they found it increasingly difficult to rule their huge empire from Rome. Communication channels were much slower back then. One could compare the travel times of that time with today's situation to get an idea of the potential challenges in space communication. The only solution at that time was to give the administrative units more autonomy and to allow them to act more decentrally. Then they did not always have to wait for new orders from Rome to be able to act. Should our modern communication also reach its time limits, this must be solved once again by technological decentralization.

Practical examples: Undoubtedly this is not really relevant yet. But let's look a little bit ahead with this topic and think about what blockchain can be used for not only today but perhaps in a few decades. There may of course be other alternative technologies available that make blockchain redundant (more on this later). Nevertheless for me it's always exciting to think about what might come next and what would be necessary for it. Winners anticipate, losers react. Therefore, always think about what other applications might be relevant and innovative and would actually benefit from a decentralized solution. Hopefully you have the decisive idea that will forever change the world for the better.

ENTREPRENEURSHIP
(STARTUPS, FOUNDING A COMPANY...)

Problem description: If you look at entrepreneurship in the online sector, you can see just how easy it is for just about everyone to start their own business, even for a young person in a garage. The costs are usually limited to an own computer and Internet connection. This also explains how the incredible boom in online businesses has taken place in recent years. The opposite is the case in many hardware industries, which usually require millions or even billions of USD in initial investment to get started. In between there are many entrepreneurial areas which could actually be founded with very little capital, but which are often not possible due to other factors such as trust, law or morality.

Solution explanation: While the law and morals are not quite as simple to approach, trust can be created excellently through a blockchain. We have already discussed many of the application areas. In this section, however, I would like to stress once again how drastic the changes will be for entrepreneurs in the future if a blockchain can create confidence, a requirement that previously cost huge amounts of money. Suddenly a 14-year-old can start a revolutionary bank from his or her room; a person in a remote and not very trustworthy country can start a trustworthy pharmaceutical company or a student can completely revolutionize the audit system.

Whenever a monopoly is broken up, competition stimulates business. This is exactly what blockchain technology will enable for the entire division in numerous fields. How the Internet first led to the creation of millions of companies in the field of communications the same will happen by blockchain on the field of trust.

Challenges: As with the Internet, blockchain technology will take time to achieve the expected victory. Entrepreneurs must first learn to create good applications through decentralization in order to create benefits for their customers.

Alternative possibilities: There are no alternatives to the often better solution, which is a blockchain. So it will only be a matter of time before we hear about the next 19-year-old who has created the next Unicorn, a company worth over 1 billion USD, in the student dormitory - only this time not in the Internet area, but in the blockchain area.

Practical examples: Since the boom of the Internet, there has never been such a boom in business startups as with decentralized applications. Even if there are still very few real successes today, it is enough if only one percent of them succeed to change the world forever. Blockchain will revolutionize entrepreneurship at least as much as the Internet did before. Blockchain technology offers a platform for simplifying an otherwise complex process: building trust.

I have now introduced over 100 of the most innovative blockchain 2.0 applications of the Post-Bitcoin era. In a later chapter, I will go into more detail on how you can go from your idea to implementation and then hopefully to success. Before that, however, I would like to tame your enthusiasm a little and show you some potential dangers for the blockchain technology, which could unfortunately destroy or slow it down.

SEVEN THREATS TO BLOCKCHAIN TECHNOLOGY

Now that we have mainly talked about the blockchain and all its advantages, we have talk about the threats. This is particularly important: there is no point in just talking euphorically about a topic and simply not recognizing or admitting that dangers exist. For clarification, just because I'm pointing them out doesn't mean I don't believe in blockchain. On the contrary, I firmly believe in the triumph of this technology. Nevertheless, only if you know your „opponent" well, you can defeat him.

1. HYPE

One of the biggest dangers for blockchain in general is the often mentioned misleading marketing. Some blockchain initiatives just don't know any better. Instead of promoting decentralization, they only harm the idea of blockchain through an excessive hype. One of the best-known and most striking examples is that of „Long Island Ice Tea", a company that has renamed itself „Blockchain Ice Tea" for marketing reasons. The price of the share of the company doubled overnight only because of the Hype name „Blockchain". It was then followed by a lot of negative press and a hefty penalty from the Stock Exchange Commission (SEC).

Such examples are reminiscent of the time of the dot-com bubble in the 90s. Even then, companies praised completely worthless technology as a model for success in order to achieve short-term profit.

Unfortunately, this is the same in the blockchain area. Almost sectarian fans are looking for more blockchain projects. This often leads to the advertising of a product or service that does not require a blockchain. The offensive advertising with the word „blockchain" brings project operators a short-term profit. This then leads to partly justified criticism in the media and to uncertainty among the rest of the population and companies which would otherwise be quite open to the blockchain issue.

The only solution for this is correct marketing of all participants and a focus on the longevity and sustainability of the blockchain projects. This is exactly what we stand for at #CRYPTOFIT. We should all rebuke all those project initiators who are highly aggressive in spreading half-truths and thus harming the entire industry.

2. SCANDALS

There will always be setbacks in this innovative area. But the entire community has to take care that these don't lead to scandals. Such scandals can be used by the press to proactively counteract blockchain technology. Some things can be actively influenced here. However, a Black Swan event, such as a terrorist attack made possible by blockchain, would be a horror scenario not only for those affected, but for the entire industry. If and how such things can be prevented can often only be thought through in theory. In practice, things usually turn out differently. Many scandals come from the area of cryptocurrencies, which is the reason they are seen rather negatively even though the topic blockchain is seen rather positively especially in business circles. Of course you can say that there is no such thing as bad press. As long as a subject only attracts attention, that's good. In order not to harm the entire industry, however, cryptocurrencies should try to act as best they can within the legal framework on the one hand, and the other blockchain applications on the other hand should try to prevent the bad branding from spilling over.

3. REGULATION

A danger that is mentioned again and again in blockchain is the threat of a ban at some point or over-regulation by countries or governments.

This argument cannot be dismissed: since decentralization can be a threat to centralization, banks and regulators are presumably very interested in suppressing it. However, this logic is based on a big misunderstanding. Governments love blockchains because they provide an incredible number of benefits: transparency, clarity, interoperability, speed, etc.

Almost everyone is interested in making positive progress in this area. However, they also see the potential dangers and do not know how to deal with them yet. If a country would really try to ban blockchains, the result would be exactly the same as in countries that have banned the Internet: a bad reputation of their economy and the flight of talented people to countries where blockchains can be used. Not a desirable result.

Often one hears with blockchain regulation the possibility of a censorship of the Internet. Without the Internet, people could not have decentralized communication. So is it a danger for blockchains that someone turns off or censors the Internet in order not to destroy a blockchain directly, but to prevent it? Apart from the fact that it is very difficult to shut down the Internet as the largest decentralized system ever, think about how many applications that are vital for daily use of the Internet. Even if a government was able to censor certain accesses, the open source apps could immediately switch to alternative ports. In addition, so-called mesh networks would emerge, which would act like the peer-to-peer networks mentioned earlier. People can get information via peers through bluetooth and direct wireless connections instead of servers and routers. A group of the Bitcoin community is even considering sending special satellites into space to ensure the independence and sustainability of blockchains. Even if the danger of a ban is omnipresent, many activists in this field try to contain this danger as far as possible.

4. QUANTUM COMPUTERS

A blockchain creates the necessary trust through cryptography. If this cryptography fails, there will be no more trust in this technology. If the cryptography should break, then you could hack a blockchain. If today the press wrongly talks about a 'blockchain hack', it means that a private key has been stolen or the database of a cryptocurrency exchange has been hacked. However, the blockchain itself was not hacked. Quantum computers could actually hack a blockchain. These are gigantic computers which can recalculate the cryptographic algorithms. This would allow them to identify a private key from the public key - and any protection would be made redundant, and they could actually hack a blockchain. But: while this scenario can occur in theory, it doesn't look that gloomy in practice. Already today quantum computer resistant cryptographies are used, which could also be implemented in blockchains. Moreover, in such a case not only blockchains would have a problem, but also the entire Internet, which is also largely based on the same cryptography. In the event that it becomes known that a computer could „crack" the code, this would initially result in a sharp drop in confidence. The protocol for restoring the blockchain would then have to be adapted in order to restore the lost trust. Quantum computers are therefore a real danger for blockchains. From today's point of view, however, it can be said that the problems caused by them could be solved.

5. ARTIFICIAL INTELLIGENCE

The danger posed by Artificial Intelligence (AI) has already been discussed in the chapter on Skynet. It goes without saying that a blockchain combined with AI, could destroy itself. That would be an interesting paradox: a danger, which only arises from what it poses a danger to. Without blockchain, AI couldn't become a Skynet in the first place.

Only through blockchain does this possibility exist at all. Luckily, we're still a little away from even creating a generalized AI. So I don't worry too much about this threat yet.

6. ALTERNATIVE TECHNOLOGIES

I will go into this point in more detail in the next chapter. Therefore, only for the sake of clarity, will I mark out a few aspects of this danger at this point. The main shortcoming of a blockchain is that everyone has to know everything. The speed and computing power of a node is the limit for the entire blockchain. If the node in question cannot process more than 100 updates per second, this is the maximum capacity of the entire blockchain - otherwise there is no consensus in this system. However, many systems would require thousands of updates per second. Some more recent approaches therefore move in the direction that consensus no longer has to prevail in the entire system. Such technologies as Directed Acyclic Graphs (DAGs), including the Tangle, or Gossip-on-Gossip protocols, and the Hashgraph, can be regarded as a serious threat or competitor to blockchain technology. However, this point of view must be treated with caution, as both concepts are not in an actual phase of use yet. From today's perspective, blockchains are more likely to prevail than alternative technologies, even though there will be some interesting innovations to come. If you want to know more about these technologies, just type „Julian Hosp IOTA" and „Julian Hosp Hashgraph" in Google.

7 . BENEVOLENT DICTATOR

Blockchain technology has its raison d'être mainly because we do not trust a centralized system. If, however, a centralized system was indeed to be fully trusted, blockchains, including their applications, would be practically unnecessary. A decentralized system is costly and sometimes brings slower speed, a lack of responsibility and rigidness with it - all things we are doing to compromise on decentralization. A blockchain enables the community to maintain control without having to trust anyone else. What blockchains could destroy is the full confidence of a community in a centralized power. But how possible is it to get a benevolent dictator who has complete control and yet enjoys all the trust of society?

Personally I don't see anything and nobody who combines both opposites in himself in the near future. Even if such a benevolent dictator would be the blockchain killer par excellence, I am convinced that decentralized systems in future will just have as great a place in society as the Internet has today.

BLOCKCHAIN ALTERNATIVES

We have already got to know blockchain alternatives briefly in the application examples and also in the part about the dangers. Here I would like to comment on the two most relevant at the moment. The benevolent dictator undoubtedly remains the most relevant alternative; yet decentralization is the much-needed counterpart to such centralization - but it remains to be seen whether blockchain technology or one of the opponents will ultimately win the race. However, the question is important. Because if you start out in a decentralized world today, you don't want to get the wrong horse into a decentralized race. So let's look at the alternatives and consider both the pros and cons of each system.

DIRECTED ACYCLIC GRAPH (TANGLE...)

Directed Acyclic Graphs (DAGs) such as IOTA's Tangle and many others are often described as an extended blockchain. However, this is not really correct. In mathematics, such net-like structures have existed for longer than the concept of a blockchain. It is simply a question of their access to consensus building. If one imagines a village, then centralization, blockchain, DAG and the Gossip-on-Gossip protocol explained in detail in the next section are easy to understand. In centralization, there is a chief in the village to whom everyone must go if he wants new information confirmed as a fact, such as two people had a hanky-panky last night. If the chief agrees, then so be it. If he refuses, there is no chance of ever integrating an event as a fact. All the villagers trust the chief and take over his knowledge without ifs or buts. Such a system is fast, easy to update, and there can never be any misunderstandings, because a single person is in charge.

In the case of a blockchain, at least 51 percent of the village must be convinced that the hanky-panky has taken place. The remaining 49 percent then adopt this opinion. The updates take place in certain time blocks. But because everyone in the village must always be kept on the same level, not many updates can happen at the same time. Because that would confuse everyone, and sometimes it could come to a completely divided opinion, i.e. a fork. A single villager can't become a tyrant for that. In addition, an outsider could come into the village and ask: „Can I have a complete overview of who has ever had a hanky-panky with whom in your village?" On the basis of the entire transparent overview, this question could easily be answered without the outsider having to trust anybody in particular.

A DAG goes a different way: the consensus does not require the consent of 51 percent of the villagers. As long as enough villagers confirm the hanky-panky it is seen as fact. The required value is called weight. It is created when every villager who wants to make a new update has to save several other updates. If one makes a statement as a villager now, then one sees that for example 3 percent in the village have accepted this opinion. If it was about something small, one could say that this was enough. For example, if something bigger was involved, 10 percent could be demanded.

In a DAG, it will never be that the large part has the entire knowledge, but that everybody has just a bit and trusts that everybody else also has a bit. The big advantage here is scaling. There are practically innumerable things updateable at the same time. A further advantage is that each participant assumes all roles in a decentralized system. In this way, there seem to be no fees, since no consensus algorithm that costs anything is required. However, this would contradict the statement that every decentralized system requires a cost point. Unfortunately, this point is also completely wrongly marketed by many systems using a DAG: the real reason why there are no costs is a centralized coordinator.

For most DAGs, network updates are currently free of charge (I don't think that will be the case for DAGs in the long run). Therefore, an attacker, as in a DDoS attack on the Internet (i.e. a service blockade due to server overload), could fill the DAG without spam protection with meaningless updates and thus disable it. However, a centralized coordinator intervenes as spam protection and releases every transaction initiated by a user. At the same time, he also regularly takes screenshots of the entire network, so that at certain times the entire information of the network is available to everyone. Otherwise it would be impossible for an outsider to see what really happened at a DAG because each participant has different information about the overall system.

Something that is unfortunately often seen with the DAGs is a sectarian trap often for young people who are not really aware of the advantages and disadvantages of this blockchain alternative. Its sole objective is to establish DAGs as blockchain alternatives. This often leads to irrational reactions to justified criticism, for example in the case of security analysts at the elite university MIT (Massachusetts Institute of Technology). This university wanted to highlight problems at IOTA and was then threatened by the founders of IOTA on the Internet, as can be read in the article „Someone should slap that bitch".[20]

Personally, however, I regard it as incredibly important that various working groups try to address this issue of alternative decentralized systems. Nevertheless, it has never been possible to establish such systems without a coordinator and thus make them truly decentralized. This raises the essential question of which problem a DAG tries to solve if it only functions centralized to this day. There are attempts to dis-

---

[20] https://spectrum.ieee.org/tech-talk/computing/networks/cryptographers-urge-users-and-researchers-to-abandon-iota-after-leaked-emails

able the existing coordinator. Maybe this could be a small insurance in case blockchains ever fail.

My own companies continue to build on blockchain technology, even if we could switch to other options. From today's point of view I dare to say that DAGs have a right to be there, but are definitely no blockchain substitutes. DAGs are therefore more likely to be used for special cases in the future. The Tangle from IOTA, for example, could be used by some companies very well with IoT devices within a controlled system. Here it would be perfectly okay for a centralized coordinator to exist, namely the company itself. I consider it unlikely that the token will spread to all areas at the same time, because every company can simply copy this token and would not need to use the token of the other company and trust the coordinator of the other company. If you look at the number of projects alone, you can see that considerably more companies worldwide rely on blockchain than on DAG, although both technologies have existed long enough.

It is simply not clear yet how a DAG should be kept decentralized and whether a centralized system might not function better than a DAG.

Of course, this is my personal assessment of the future. I have made numerous highly detailed videos on DAGs and IOTA, which you should watch if you are interested in this topic. As I said, maybe this technology fits your specific application.

Search the Internet for „Julian Hosp IOTA" and you will find many helpful videos and blog entries.

GOSSIP ON GOSSIP (HASHGRAPH…)

The second blockchain alternative is also based on a well-known mathematical model built on gossip-on gossip-principals. Here we try to combine the advantages of decentralizing a blockchain with the scalability of a DAG. Based on the village example, this works by installing an indirect reputation system in the village. When one hears gossip from one person and this gossip is independently confirmed by more and more people, then one begins to trust the person sharing the rumor more and more. So no majority is required to create a fact, but the gossip moves agilely through the village. The reputation model thus seeks to replace the centralized coordinator of a DAG.

Such a model seems to work theoretically, but it has never been tested in reality. The company Hedra, which seeks to establish a patent for its technology of the Hashgraph, is currently the only one active in this field. It will be questionable, above all, how such a commercialized system can be in an environment that is actually open source dominated. Moreover, it is not clear yet whether the game theoretical principles of the Gossip-on-Gossip reputation model can also be implemented in practice.

Similar to DAGs, I also see potential in this protocol. In my opinion, however, it will rather establish itself in special fields and not be a triumphal march as an entire technology. It's simply a misconception to think that innovation can win only because of its technology - it's much more about usability, security and stability. The sometimes quite primitive construct of the Internet proves this again and again. If you want more detailed information about Gossip-on-Gossip protocols, search the Internet for „Julian Hosp Hashgraph".

Form your own opinion from all the introduced advantages and disadvantages of blockchain, DAG and Gossip-on-Gossip in any case, also by dealing intensively with the strengths and weaknesses. Does it seem advisable to invest time, money and energy in one or the other? Fathoming this is essential - not only because the next chapter gives you a quick guide on how to get started in this area, but because dealing with these things can shape the future of your company, your family or your legacy.

ENTREPRENEURSHIP: FROM THEORY TO IMPLEMENTATION

> *It doesn't matter whether the glass is half full or half empty, as an entrepreneur you think about how you can sell the glass.*

This chapter, as the quote describes, is about preparing your company for the time of decentralization by identifying lucrative problems, creating profitable solutions and implementing them. Don't make the mistake that many company founders make when they believe that an idea alone is worth a lot. Pretty much every idea has already been produced once - only its implementation is what brings money. But before we start with the right idea for the solution, let's go back to the beginning and start with the problem.

FROM PROBLEM TO SOLUTION

Perhaps through this book you have realized how important this wave of innovation is. Then now is the time to do something about it, either through your existing business, your new startup, or perhaps even, if you hold a publicly exposed position, to optimally orient your state towards decentralization. You've pretty much just experienced all the potential problems and solutions from today's perspective. Now is the time for action.

So start again with the problem: 6 + 4 = ?

Just think about the following questions:

- What disturbs you in general in everyday life? Could the point in question bother anyone else?
- In your opinion, which services do you spend money on unnecessarily?
- Which services need unnecessary time?
- Where in your existing company can you find processes that are incredibly inefficient due to trust problems?
- Where have you ever heard from friends or acquaintances that there is a trust problem during a process?

Ask yourself these questions really regularly. If you want, get my bestseller "25 Stories I would tell my younger self" on Amazon. Here I explain strategies how you can easily recognize such problems with only five minutes a day and use them for yourself. The book is so popular among entrepreneurs for a reason - I really put all my business knowledge into it.

If you now have identified a problem for yourself that you would like to address, the next question arises.

BLOCKCHAIN OR CENTRALIZED DATABASE?

The question of whether the solution should be implemented with or without blockchain is incredibly relevant. Because not all problems need a blockchain as a solution, as you have noticed in the different applications. If you want to be active in the blockchain area, which I can recommend because of the future prospects, the choice of the tool is crucial.

In 2014, I actually wanted to found a blockchain startup in the medical field, but it just didn't fit. I had stay flexible, and ended up in the financial sector. You can find out how relevant an area is for blockchain in the 'Practical Applications' section of this book. If you want to, you can also use this flowchart to come to a decision:
https://medium.com/@sbmeunier/when-do-you-need-blockchain-decision-models-a5c40e7c9ba1

Of course, the graphics aren't to be taken completely

seriously, but nevertheless it shows quite clearly that more often than not, dismissing a blockchain is the better solution than using it.

If you have come to the conclusion that you need a blockchain to solve your problem, you are faced with the question of whether you want to set it up completely on your own or whether you would rather build upon an existing one.

A little tip from my side: nowadays you can start almost all use cases on already existing blockchains at least as a proof of concept at extremely low cost. This must also be the goal: an MVP (Minimum Viable Prototype), which validates your idea and speaks clearly for solving a problem in your way. The procedure is different, depending on whether you are the founder of your own company, an employee in an existing company, or a person responsible for a public organization.

BLOCKCHAIN IN STARTUPS

Being a founder in your own startup company is the dream of many - maybe even yours? Let's take a look at the functional process if you want to start your own startup:

1. **Solution:** Everything starts with the optimal solution for a real existing problem. No hype, no farce, but something that people or machines would really

use. You'll realize pretty quickly that the pure ideas are pretty worthless. In this book alone I speak of over 100 possible applications. If you manage to implement only one of them, you can create a benefit for millions of people and earn billions.

2. **Team:** A good blockchain startup team consists of the three Hs: Hacker, Hipster and Hustler. The hacker can program. The hipster is the designer. The hustler takes care of partnerships and marketing. Sometimes only two people cover the three Hs, but I have never seen one person unite all the Hs. So you're gonna need one or more partners. You may have to look for them first, and it may take a while. Just don't be upset! Once you've got your core team, which usually consists of generalists, you'll have to hire specialists as quickly as you can who are particularly well versed in a distinct area. The more experienced and better they are in their respective specialty, the higher your chance of success. You need money for that, and that brings us to the next point.

3. **Financing:** Especially in the blockchain space you will have a hard time selling your product directly to customers at the beginning. In most cases, development takes a few years until it generates sales. So you're gonna have to learn how to raise money. There are sev-

eral possibilities, and I would like to introduce a few to you. One important point in advance: a good investor will only invest in the team and not necessarily in the idea. A good idea with a bad team is doomed to failure. A good team can make gold out of anything.

a. Angels or the three F's (Friends, Family, Fools): These are people who invest their own money in a company at a very early stage. Usually the sums involved range from 25,000 to 50,000 USD. You can also find such Angels on LinkedIn, Meetup and other events. I also invest as an angel. If you think you have a good team with all three Hs and want to tackle a blockchain problem, contact us with your pitch deck here: team@julianhosp.com. Important: Do not contact us if you are missing any of the Hs. We do not invest in ideas, but in teams.

b. Venture capitalists and funds: These investors invest other people's money professionally in promising business models. In the early stages of a startup, this usually involves sums of 50,000 to 1 million USD. You can find venture capitalists on the Internet - but make sure they are serious.

c. Crowdfunding / Initial Coin Offerings: we will discuss these in detail later, but I can recommend you to get angels or venture capitalists on board first in order to have enough capital and mentors for an Initial Coin Offering.

4. **Legal:** I could write a whole book about what is important in contracts, structures and agreements. Maybe I'll do that once in a while, but here just this: keep the most important things as clear and simple as possible at the beginning and only lose yourself in detail much later. Otherwise it will cost you unnecessary nerves, time and money.

5. **Doing:** Perhaps That is the most important point. Don't get stuck on one idea, try to get results. Stay flexible with your approach and try to get to an MVP (Minimal Viable Prototype) as fast as possible, i.e. to a first execution of your idea. If that is just a proof of concept9, it doesn't matter. Because only with implementation you will find customers, investors or other team members. You may need years without anything going on, and then suddenly success comes overnight. Don't quit your permanent job right away, but keep your job part-time at least initially. As a young entrepreneur you must be prepared that 100-hour work weeks will not be uncommon here. There would be so many other things to mention and I could

write 500 pages about this chapter alone. I don't want to get lost in details and better reserve that for another book that I might publish once. Before setting up a company, really reflect on whether you would rather join another startup company that is perhaps even working on a similar idea and has already solved some of the initial funding and other hurdles. There may be a lot less downside coming towards you, but you can still take some of that upside with you.

As a serial entrepreneur, I can recommend that you join a young startup rather than initiate one yourself. As I said, many of the hurdles mentioned have already been overcome in an existing startup compared to an imminent one, but the potential advantages can still be enormous. Personally, I see the risk-benefit ratio for a sixth employee as much more interesting than for a founder. If you, like me, are still willing to take the risks, then I will give you five tips later to become a successful entrepreneur.

Apart from a startup, of course you could start a blockchain project in your existing organization (company or public institution), which brings me to the next chapter.

BLOCKCHAIN IN AN EXISTING COMPANY OR A PUBLIC INSTITUTION

Implementing a blockchain concept as an employee or owner in your existing company follows different rules than with a startup. The very first question you should ask yourself is: how high is the risk and how high is the return of an innovation? This may surprise you a little, because normally I always emphasize that innovation should be driven forward. Nevertheless, there are a few things to consider here - which I would like to divide into three categories:

A. Small and Medium-sized Enterprise (SME): If you work in an SME or own one, you will be much more agile than a corporation or government. Your resources will be a bit scarcer and you will have to consider potential investments in terms of time or money more carefully. You won't run so much of a reputational risk here trying to integrate blockchain. Rather, you will have to count in your own input. In principle, you have some advantages compared to a new startup, because you will already have an existing customer base. For ideas, decisions, team and financing you can also build on your entrepreneurial experience. If you align your SME in a perfect way to blockchain, you will achieve an attractive risk-benefit ratio.

B. **Group/Corporation:** If you work in a larger company and want to introduce blockchain technology, you have other challenges, but also advantages over an SME. Since there are usually enough resources available here, it will be easier to initiate a blockchain project as a proof of concept. However, the big challenge here will be to convince the management of this project. Why this project and not another? Why this technology? Why the requested capital? My tip for this, which I also implement for my own company in partnerships with large corporations is „training". We offer potential partners blockchain trainings and send them some of my books about blockchain and/or cryptocurrencies. If the managers understand the dangers and potentials of this new technology, they will be self-motivated. Use tools like these lectures and books and let them build their own opinion. If you want to contact our team here, please contact us here: team@julianhosp.com. Once the management is convinced of this, it is a matter of creating a proof of concept in a subunit of the company. The primary goal here is to keep potential reputational damage caused by new technologies to a minimum. Otherwise, the risk-benefit ratio is too high on the risk side. So it's better to test things first on a small scale and only integrate them into the company later on. If there is enough capital available and a potential takeover opportunity of a startup exists, it can also be worthwhile to directly buy the know-how, team and result of another company. Of course, this has to be coordinated individually in each case. It might also help to consult a blockchain expert who protects against missteps.

C. **Government/official bodies:** Again, it is different when you work for a government, an authority or public institution. If you want to advance innovation here, you should use the same "persuasion tactics" as in a corporate group. You should also use outsiders for this persuasion work. Seldom budgets or resources play a role in public policies, but rather the establishment of precise guidelines. This is a general tip with regard to regulators, governments and other official entities: the easiest way for them to do this is if they do not have to implement such technical innovations themselves, but can provide targeted support for startups in their own region in this project. This way, the most added value is created for entrepreneurs, customers and ultimately also for the region itself. It could be a small pilot project or even a whole sandbox where startups enjoy certain advantages if they do research in the desired area. This is exactly why I am active in working groups of the EU and many other countries worldwide: I want to promote such projects in a business-friendly way, and I also want to ensure that regulation promotes the projects instead of hindering them.

Regardless of whether it is your own startup or an existing company, capital always plays an important role. Therefore, in the next chapter I will deal with one of the most innovative but at the same time controversial funding models in the blockchain space.

INITIAL COIN OFFERINGS (ICO´S)

I have mentioned the topic ICO´s again and again, albeit briefly. But in this chapter, I want to give you a few business tips. Because of our own 80 million ICO, I am internationally recognized as an ICO expert. Therefore I would like to report from my own experience about what ICO´s are, why they are relevant for you as an entrepreneur and how you can use them optimally.

An ICO or Initial Coin Offering is a way for a company or organization to create its own cryptocurrency and then publicly offer it for sale. The aforementioned new cryptocurrency can have its own blockchain, as Ethereum did in 2014, but it can also be token-based on another platform like Ethereum, for example as an ERC20 token. The latter is the most common variant. In an ICO, the buyers of the new token exchange their existing cryptocurrencies for the company's new tokens. The company receives capital, the buyer receives the token and all the benefits associated with it. Normally the new token is treated as something independent, which can increase in value or not. It is more a hope of the token buyer that the company will do with the money what it promised. Many companies that create an ICO are still in the startup phase, and so it must be understood that an ICO entails incomparably higher risks for investors. But for you as an entrepreneur, such an ICO can be quite interesting. While traditional financing methods by angels or venture capitalists are possible, the blockchain world has become accustomed to this new form of direct financing called ICOs. The advantage for the company is that it can usually get more money directly from the buyers without having to sell part of the company at the same time. The advantage for the buyer is that an ICO can be financially attractive.

In order for your ICO to be successful as an entrepreneur, you should consider a few things that we have already discussed in the startup chapter:

1. **Idea:** You need a good, solid idea that solves a real problem, not one that is not applicable.

2. **Implementation:** As I said, ideas are worth very little if there is no excellent implementation yet. I would only recommend an ICO if you already have a Minimal Viable Prototype (MVP) or other results to show.

3. **Team:** You need an existing team of developers, product people, legal experts, marketing people and many more specialists. That's why I recommend that you do an angel or seed round first and then an ICO.

4. **Token structure:** The legal and financial token structure must be set up correctly. For example, what is the maximum purchase price? How much does the token cost at the beginning? What percentage of tokens are sold? In which country does the ICO take place? What is the function of the token? There is no single correct answer to many questions. But one has to understand what is behind them and why they are put forward. Nowadays you should also ask yourself if you want to make a utility token or a security token ICO.

5. **Communication:** Marketing and communication are the key to success. This is the only factor that cannot be standardized and is always individual. This will be discussed in more detail in the next chapter, when we talk about marketing in the blockchain space.

I've done countless videos and have written many blog posts on this subject, and I strongly recommend that you search the Internet for „Julian Hosp ICO" if you're planning an ICO yourself.

MARKETING

A successful product or service always consists of two things: on the one hand, a great solution to a problem that affects many people, and on the other hand the awareness of the product or service among the people who have the problem. Awareness is achieved through marketing, which is why the relation is often described with the following formula:

$$P(roduct) = I(nnovation) + M(arketing)$$

There's nothing worse than an innovative product that is not known by anybody. Unfortunately, many entrepreneurs very often forget this fact. They sometimes spend years tinkering with a perfect solution, only to find out that nobody buys it. However, if you approach the whole thing correctly and start not with the solution, but with the problem, you should also make it much easier to find customers for it. If you don't, you're like all the others who ask me, „Julian, I developed/built XYZ. What's the best way to market this?" The developers in question sometimes find it very difficult to do this because they have not thought enough about the solution and the actual problem. A much better way to make your own product or service known is the following:

> *Problem → Target Group → Solution → Marketing → Success*

If you start with a problem, you don't have to think about a solution right away. Instead, think about who has the problem so you automatically have a target group for your offered solution. Marketing should then be relatively easy for you, because it won't be so difficult to find out which social media channels the target group in question uses, what interests they have, etc.

I'd like to recommend three more secret weapons which are especially interesting in the blockchain space:

1. **Free value:** The most powerful method in branding is not to promote your company, but to distribute free value to people. This may sound funny, but people are already so dulled by advertising that they usually subconsciously hide banners, pop ups or advertisements. Especially in as new an area blockchain, the best possibility is therefore to educate people free of charge. That's how you build your brand and people will buy a good product. If you start with that, start with a niche and not with the whole product range. It'll make it easier for you to establish yourself as an expert. In my opinion, this marketing method is the only sustainable one and it

is also the one on which I and my companies focus most strongly.

2. **Influencers:** In times when advertising is becoming increasingly expensive, it can be extremely effective to work with influencers who advertise their own product or service on YouTube, Instagram or Facebook. This can be remunerated via an affiliate commission in the future or via an advance commission. For example, I work together with Ledger and promote their wallet as an influencer, which I also use myself. Of course, it is extremely important to consider carefully which[21] influencers you are working with. I strongly recommend that you look for sustainable influencers instead of falling for short-term rip-offs. You can easily find these influencers by watching who's talking about blockchain technology on Instagram, YouTube or Facebook. If you want to promote a product or service through our platform and it is not an investment product, you can contact us here: team@julianhosp.com.

3. **Airdrops:** The last secret weapon is particularly suitable for ICO marketing when you're under time pressure. While the other two methods have proven to be more suitable for long-term market development, it is some-

---

21 www.julianhosp.com/hardwallet

times necessary to achieve effective results immediately. If you have an ICO running at the moment and want to generate short-term attention on it, you can airdrop your own token to other already successful projects. This means that you can transfer your own token free of charge to the existing token holders. In this way, they will become aware of the token, inform themselves about your ICO and possibly invest as well. Unfortunately, this version is being abused more and more. But at the moment it still seems to work sufficiently well, as I often hear from our own community.

So marketing is not witchcraft as long as you do it right and smart. Just do not try to do what everyone else does, because the measures in question are usually overpriced and inefficient.

FIVE SUCCESS CHARACTERISTICS OF AN ENTREPRENEUR

Only 20 percent of your success will result from the actual strategy and the tools described here. The really important 80 percent are your mental attitude, beliefs, motivation etc. - the so-called soft skills. If, for example, you want to know how I have acquired many of these skills over time and implemented them in the most diverse fields such as professional sports, medicine and entrepreneurship, I can recommend the following book: 25 Stories for My Younger Self.

The most important points are the following:

1. **People:** It is essential with whom you surround yourself, because you will always adapt to your environment. For you as an entrepreneur in the blockchain area, the recommendation is to surround yourself with other like-minded people. For example in good groups, masterminds etc. This was probably the most important factor with regard to my own success. You won't make it on your own; you need good people around you.

2. **Vision:** The reason why you do what you do is also decisive. When you look at a gazelle and a lion in Africa, they both wake up every morning. However, they do so for different reasons: The gazelle because it is afraid to be eaten, the lion because it wants to hunt. So learn not to let yourself be driven by fear, but by positive attitude. Create a great vision that will inspire you to work on creating amazing things. My vision, for example, is to make one billion people in the world #cryptofit and thus leaving a great legacy. I have no idea if I will ever be

able to do that, but it motivates me to do my best as often as I can.

3. **Growth:** It is essential to understand that you will never finish learning. You have to grow constantly by continuing your education and accepting new challenges again and again. This is easier if you have a good group of people around you and are driven by a great vision.

4. **Execution:** All the things described above are of no use to you if you do not execute on them to full extent. Talent is not the basis, but the peak of success. Many unsuccessful people unfortunately use the excuse of allegedly lacking talents all too often. They attribute other people's success primarily to their talent or happiness. But the reality is different: for example, if you throw 100 spaghetti on the wall, one of them will almost certainly stick to it. You don't know which one before, but if you throw enough, one will stick. In life you have to try as many things as possible for your success. Don't be discouraged by missteps, but quite the opposite: consider them as necessary steps on the stairs to success.

5. **Inspiration:** Become an inspiration for other peo-

ple. Whether it's getting investment money, attracting employees or getting customers, you will have to inspire others with your vision and your actions. The attitude of giving without expecting helps enormously here: who gives without immediately thinking about what he gets for it, has it easier.

All these points concern you as a person - no matter whether you work in an existing company or want to start your own, whether you work for the government or are still a student, whether you are only 18 or already 50. The dots are universal, and you should memorize them and consider them as indispensable rules to your success. .

THE FUTURE OF DECENTRALIZATION

In the coming years, it will probably become increasingly clear that neither centralization nor decentralization alone will be the ultimate solution. Decentralization is the necessary counterbalance to the current omnipresent centralization. It thus creates a balance which we are heading towards in the coming years. Even though decentralization is an outstanding principle, I do not believe that it is the only way forward.

Blockchains, decentralization and all resulting applications are so important precisely because they give people a choice. You can continue to use the centralized services, but you don't have to. Some centralized organizations will see exactly that. They will understand, that they need to offer their users the best of both worlds, if they want to continue to have a raison d'être. There will be a need for centralized institutions, but decentralized communities will challenge them. They have to be in top form and can't just do what they want. Nobody wants absolute chaos, but nobody wants a monarchy or a dictatorship. It's about finding the golden middle. It won't be 50-50. Rather, it is a matter of producing an optimal mix of 100 percent centralized and 100 percent decentralized systems. What exactly this mix looks like will become apparent in the future. All the other companies that do not accept this innovation will go bankrupt in these years. All those companies that embrace and build on this movement will flourish incredibly, just as the companies who have embraced the Internet revolution.

I believe that we will soon be communicating with a neuro-linked brain with confidence via various blockchains. Through machine learning, the system selects how we tap the trust and then use it. All of this will take place fully automatically, without having to actively concentrated on it. Gold, real estate, wealth, identity or many other things will be completely seamless in this way, without any friction, immediately and securely compatible with each other - all over the world and perhaps also on other planets.

I know a lot of this still sounds crazy today. But that's exactly what we thought 30 years ago about mobile phones, social media or free video telephony. The same applies to this new revolution in information storage through blockchains. By reading this book you have laid your personal foundation for the decentralized revolution of blockchain 2.0. The first step into a new territory is always the scariest. So I want to thank you for trusting me to make this move with you. I'd also like to congratulate you on embarking on this journey. You are now really #CRYPTOFIT and ready for all the exciting things that the world of decentralization has to offer. Much in this area is moving at enormous speed, and even while I was writing this book, new possibilities

THE FUTURE OF DECENTRALIZATION

have arisen. As a quick reminder: exclusively for readers of this book, I have an up-to-date list with details, videos, blogs and further literature. Furthermore you can find all links from this publication there. If you want to use this information as a free bonus to the book, then go on: www.morethanjustbitcoin.com and get the latest version.

AFTERWORD

Congratulations, you have made it! Now you have not only an overview of blockchain and how this technology can be used and how it will affect our lives, but you are absolutely and even more than just #CRYPTOFIT. You may be wondering what your next steps should be. Here is a little to-do list for you:

1. Think about what problems you have regularly in your daily life. Have a little list ready where you write it down, what you notice.

2. Be creative and think about whether there is a solution based on a blockchain.

3. If you want to have some deeper insights and see how I apply these things, have a look at this exclusive VIP webinar: www.julianhosp.com/englishvipwebinar

AFTERWORD

If you are not connected to me on social media yet, then do this now:

Facebook: www.facebook.com/julianhosp
Twitter: www.twitter.com/julianhosp
LinkedIn: www.linkedin.com/in/julianhosp
YouTube: www.youtube.com/julianhosp
Instagram: www.instagram.com/julianhosp

If you need me or someone from our team to give a lecture, or if you'd like to book a consulting for your company, government or group, please contact us at:
team@julianhosp.com

One last thing. If you've taken advantage of this book then help me with my vision to help people all over the world become more than just #CRYPTOFIT. Share this book with a few friends. Give it to someone for their birthday or Christmas. Put up the Amazon link on Facebook or Twitter. Please also rate this book on Amazon. It only takes a minute, but it helps others to find the book and recognize how important this topic is for them.

Remember, knowledge is only potential power. If you have read up to this point but you don't put what you've learned into practice, it's like you've never learned it. So become active and put your new knowledge into practice. Recognize the waves and ride them!

When people ask me what I see as the meaning of life, I answer: „It's about creating options, not just for me but also for others". For me, having options is synonymous with personal independence. #CRYPTOFIT means that billions of people worldwide will be able to decide whether they'd rather stay in a centralized world, or whether they want to leave for another, better option one day. It matters to me: to know that you can, not that you have to.

With this final passage I would like to thank you for being on this path with me. I wish you lots of opportunities, health, love and much success in all your actions. I hope to see you, to meet somewhere in person, or at least to hear from you by e-mail.

Keep rocking and stay (more than) #CRYPTOFIT!

Yours, Julian

Feedback on the book: www.julianhosp.com

ABOUT THE AUTHOR

Photograph by Blitzkneisser

Dr. Julian Hosp, born in 1986, is a professional sportsman, doctor, entrepreneur, blockchain expert, speaker and bestselling author.

Julian was a professional kite surfer for almost ten years and was among the top 10 in the world. 2011 he wrote the no. one reference book called KiteTricktionary.

After his high school days in Nashville, Tennessee, USA, he pursued his medical studies in Innsbruck. After graduating, he actually wanted to become an accident surgeon but after trying out life at the hospital for a moment he decided to pursue his entrepreneurial dreams.

In 2015 he published his experiences at that time with the bestseller 25 Stories I would tell my Younger Self followed by the German book Grenzenlos Erfolgreich in 2017 (The English version Be Successful Beyond Limits will be published in 2019).

ABOUT THE AUTHOR

In 2015, he became co-founder of a Singapore based fintech startup. Julian also became one of the best blockchain and cryptocurrency experts of the world. He is a frequent invited keynote speaker at events around the world and a regular guest on television and radio as well as interview partner in print media about the current blockchain trends, the future of cryptocurrencies and entrepreneurship.

Julian lives today with his wife Bettina in Singapore, but is much for business and partly private purposes all over the world on the road. All updates and further information can be found at his website and the most popular social media channels:

www.julianhosp.com

FURTHER LITERATURE

CRYPTOCURRENCIES SIMPLY EXPLAINED

www.julianhosp.com/books/cryptosimplyexplained
208 pages , ISBN: 978-9-88148-508-3

Bitcoin, blockchain and cryptocurrencies are nearly common daily in the media, but what is actually behind all this? Buzzwords? Who wants to get acquainted, stands immediately before the largest challenge, namely the question: „Where do I even start?" **This bestseller has now sold over 100,000 copies worldwide and has been translated into more than ten languages.** In his bestseller, Julian Hosp, one of the best-known blockchain and cryptocurrency experts of the world, summarizes the fundamental knowledge about digital currencies compact for beginners together - starting with the blockchain technology up to the ICOs (Initial Coin Offerings). It shows what can be done in the course of digitization and decentralization are coming to the people and what technologies have the potential to change the world in a way, as the Internet has done over the past 20 years.

25 STORIES I WOULD TELL MY YOUNGER SELF

www.julianhosp.com/books/25stories
358 Seiten, ISBN: 978-9-88148-503-8

"This book motivates anyone to find their purpose in life!"

Are you feeling a bit lost and looking for new inspiration? Have you always wanted to find true motivation in your life? Do you love reading exciting real experiences of successful people?

In this book bestselling author Dr. Julian Hosp tells 25 encouraging, but also shocking stories from his life, how he found answers to all these questions and which 75 essential lessons he would give to a younger self today, to reach the goal of financial freedom much faster.

He talks about dazzling parties and all the experiences of ten years of professional kitesurfing around the world and what that means to him today.

He takes the reader into the decision as to why he studied medicine, but did not work as a doctor and whether he regrets that in retrospect.

He describes his first businesses in his childhood and how they made it possible for him to become a serial entrepreneur today.

And he breaks down the details of how he became a millionaire out of debt in just a few years and how he would make it even faster today.

FURTHER LITERATURE

As a quick reminder: exclusively for readers of this book, I have an up-to-date list with details, videos, blogs and further literature. Furthermore you can find all links from this publication there. If you want to use this information as a free bonus to the book, then go on: www.morethanjustbitcoin.com and get the latest version.

www.ingramcontent.com/pod-product-compliance
Lightning Source LLC
Chambersburg PA
CBHW020630220526
45464CB00001B/85